STRATEGIC MANAGEMENT AND PLANNING
IN THE PUBLIC SECTOR

Forthcoming titles in the public sector management series

Accruals accounting in the public sector by V. Archibald

Managing change in the new public sector by R. Lovell

Purchasing in Government by P. Behan

Marketing in the new public sector by L. Titman

Strategic management and planning in the public sector

by
Robert J. Smith

LONGMAN

Published by Longman in association with
The Civil Service College.

STRATEGIC MANAGEMENT AND PLANNING IN THE PUBLIC SECTOR

Published by Longman Information and Reference, Longman Group Limited, 6th Floor, Westgate House, The High, Harlow Essex CM20 IYR, England and Associated Companies throughout the world.

A catalogue record for this book is available from The British Library.

ISBN 0-582-23892-7

Printed and bound in Great Britain by Bookcraft (Bath) Ltd.

Contents

Author's Foreword

The Longman/Civil Service College series of texts on Management in the Public Sector covers many of the most important topics on the current management agenda, in central Government and in the public sector as a whole. In the past many of these topics may have been the preserve of specialists. Finance was for Finance Division, human resource issues were for the Personnel Group, contracts were for Contracts Branch. Increasingly all managers, at senior, middle and junior management levels, find themselves drawn into these, previously specialist, topics. With flatter management structures and increased delegation, all managers need a broad understanding of a range of management topics. This series of books has been produced with their needs in mind.

The texts are intended to be straightforward to understand, to provide a good summary of current understanding and best practice, and to illustrate the key points with examples from the public sector. There will still be room for the specialist, but these texts should enable every manager to talk intelligently with the specialist and understand him or her better.

The very term 'strategic management' signifies that the topic is for every manager, not for a specialist, whereas strategic planning may have been seen by many as the province of a specialist department. Nevertheless there are many techniques with a specialist aura. In this book I have tried as far as possible to demystify these techniques and to concentrate on explaining how and where each technique might be helpful. The book also offers a framework to help managers to identify the key stages in the strategic management process and how they can fit together. It is hoped that this will be of interest to managers at all levels and that it will encourage them to aim to be more strategic in their management.

The ideas in this book owe much to my colleagues at the Civil Service College. Discussions with them have stimulated me to sort out my own thinking but have also generated ideas which I have somewhat unashamedly borrowed. Thanks go most particularly to John Ambrose, Tim Moorey, Lionel Titman and Brian Whalley. I would also like to thank Kerry Johnston, Alison Graham and Bob Pike for their work in producing the printed text and Andrea Drewett and colleagues in the College library for their help with the research. Any errors found in the book remain my own responsibility.

Robert J. Smith

Sunningdale

October 1994

Chapter 1

The purposes of planning and some key principles

It is all very well in theory, but .....

There are many propositions with which few people have the courage to disagree. The proposition that strategic planning is, in theory, helpful, useful, beneficial, has, at least until recently, come into that category. However, in practice it is not difficult to find people and organisations whose commitment to strategic planning appears less than total.

Plan? Why bother?

Is it really worth the time and effort? Managers in the public sector are not alone in questioning the merits of longer-term planning in particular. Personal experience in the public sector, particularly within central Government, suggests that the most commonly heard reasons for not planning can be summarised in the following two paraphrases:

- there is never time to plan because of the pressure of urgent day-to-day work
- there is little point in planning because the future is too uncertain and circumstances can change at a stroke.

It is only too easy to dismiss these 'reasons' as nothing more than excuses. However, a look at some past examples of approaches to planning could suggest that they may be justified, at least in part.

There are examples of heavily centralised planning systems which require line managers to submit large volumes of data to the planning department. The outcome is a weighty tome which appears to have little relevance to the day-to-day issues facing individual managers and which therefore sits on a shelf gathering dust. (Of course this may not apply to the most senior managers; if they have bookcases their volumes will at least not gather dust!) There are also examples of plans which have attempted to set out definitive paths for the future

1

but which have soon been overtaken by events. This situation may have arisen from doomed attempts to extrapolate past trends into the future, from a failure to recognise all of the possibilities for change, or because change was imposed from outside, for example as the result of a change in ownership or, in the public sector, a change in political control. However, planning ought not to be remote from line managers or unrealistically definitive in the decade of the 1990s, with its emphases on delegation, empowerment and flexibility.

The starting point, when seeking to identify appropriate approaches to planning, is to clarify what we wish to achieve through planning. The main purposes of planning, it is suggested, may be summarised as:

- clarity of purpose
- unity of purpose
- achievement of purpose
- framework for day-to-day decision making.

Clarity of purpose

In recent years a good deal of effort has been devoted to the development of performance indicators throughout the public sector. Experience of the provision of both training courses and consultancy has shown that problems in developing performance indicators stem more often than not from the lack of clear objectives. In turn the lack of clear objectives is often indicative of a failure to resolve some key issues about the purpose and direction of an organisation. Clarity of purpose requires a sense of direction, a set of priorities and an understanding of common values.

❏ Sense of direction

In the case of museums, what relative importance should be attached to visitor numbers, visitor satisfaction, conservation and scholarship? If considerable weight is to be given to 'scholarship', what do people understand by that term? Is the emphasis on the number of publications, the quality of publications, the volume of research funds obtained, or on peer assessment of the quality of research? Turning to prisons, to what extent should the regime be designed for punishment and the deterrence of crime, to what extent should it be geared to rehabilitation? These are the types of issues which a planning process should seek to clarify, with the conclusions expressed under headings such as:

- mission statement
- our role

- our aims
- our purpose.

❏ Priorities

Statements of mission, role, aims or purpose are quite likely to embrace, often implicitly rather than explicitly, a number of dimensions. In the case of payment of any type of grant, benefit or pension, there will be dimensions of promptness, accuracy, courtesy, efficiency or cost of administration, feedback to policy makers on the practical implications of policy options, and perhaps the outcome (eg what is achieved by the recipient as a result of the award.) Which of these dimensions should have the prime claim upon the awarding organisation's attention and effort over the planning period? Similarly, in the case of a public library, once agreement is reached on underlying purposes such as education, leisure and information services, there will be questions of priority. Should more be done to build the video library, should the range of books be increased or should resources be devoted to buying large numbers of the most popular titles? Or should the telephone information service be expanded?

The planning process should identify where improvements and changes are most needed. The outcome may well be reflected to some degree in the mission state-ments, or descriptions of role, aims and purpose mentioned above. However, it is likely to be most evident in statements such as those of:

- objectives
- key or critical success factors.

❏ Common values

A large private sector company with a number of subsidiaries would not normally restrict its interest in the strategies of those subsidiaries to financial profit. It will be interested in which products and markets they seek to expand and what types of acquisitions and divestments they wish to make, because it will wish to ensure that, corporately, the company has a sensible portfolio of products and markets. Recognising that the actions of one subsidiary can easily have impacts on another, it will also be concerned about each subsidiary's marketing and image with the consumer, and with its reputation as an employer and in the community (for example, as a contributor to local community projects).

Within the public sector as well there will be concern not only with outputs but with how they are achieved. There are some values which need to be shared across the sector. The most obvious ones are financial probity, and fairness in dealing with customers, contractors, recruitment and promotion. Public sector organisations would also be expected to set an example in complying with both the letter and the spirit of employment legislation. Perhaps these are so obvious that they can be taken as read and do not need addressing in the planning process. However, there are other issues concerning values which certainly do need to be addressed. For the future is the need for an entrepreneurial spirit or for a safe pair of hands? The answer will depend on the direction which an organisation wishes to take. Entrepreneurial flair may be valued in those seeking to encourage foreign companies to locate plants in the United Kingdom, but would be less welcome amongst those responsible for health and safety matters. Is it the wish to encourage individual initiative or teamwork or both, in which case how are the two to be reconciled? Conclusions about the values to be encouraged are likely to emerge in statements of:

- core values
- competences.

Unity of purpose

It hardly needs to be said that, however clear the mission statement, the corporate objectives and the core values, their impact on the success of an organisation is likely to be small if commitment to them is limited to the top management team! Johnson and Scholes (1984) put the point succinctly:

> Strategic changes are seldom made as a result of senior management decisions alone. It is much more usual for strategy to evolve as a result of the activities, perceptions and influence of many other individuals including the different levels of management. Furthermore, when it comes to the implementation of strategy, the chances of success without all levels of management understanding the strategic issues involved is a formula for disaster.

Ultimately success will depend on the actions of many individuals and will only be delivered if these individuals share the purpose and are sufficiently committed to it to allow their actions to be guided by it. It is suggested here that there are three key elements to achieving that commitment, participation, building knowledge of the business and its environment, and a coherent structure of plans and sub-plans. The first two elements are particularly closely related.

❑ Participation

A distinction is often drawn between top-down and bottom-up planning. An extreme example of a top-down plan would be where a chief executive produces the plan alone. It may be radical and visionary but it carries the risk that, to those ultimately delivering the service to the customer, it appears quite unrealistic or impractical. Faced by 'reality' they could well continue to act as they always have done. A second risk is that, even if realistic and practical, the priorities may not be shared by key managers and staff. They may then, either actively or passively, but certainly effectively, undermine the chief executive's intentions.

Moving to the other extreme, a purely bottom-up plan could be produced by asking individual staff or groups of staff what they would like and adding all of those ideas together. Sometimes these ideas can be very radical but, because of a narrow perspective, quite unrealistic, particularly in terms of the resources required. Alternatively they may reflect a desire to avoid any change, and this could be equally unrealistic by failing to acknowledge the strength of the external pressures for change.

It is not difficult to spot that some merging of top-down and bottom-up is required, as explained by Bryson (1988):

> Effective strategy formulation can be top-down or bottom-up. The organizations that are best at strategic planning indeed seem to combine these two approaches into an effective strategic planning system. Usually some sort of overall strategic guidance is given at the top, but detailed strategy formulation and implementation typically occur deeper in the organization. Detailed strategies and their implementation may then be reviewed at the top for consistency across strategies and with organizational purposes.

This principle is embraced in the suggestions later in this book on the conduct of a planning process. The key point at this stage is that it helps to build commitment through allowing key managers to contribute to the strategies. This does not guarantee at the end of the day that everyone can agree. There may be conflicting ideas. Top management then has to reconcile these or choose between them. That may generate a need for uncomfortable decisions about the future role of those managers who lack commitment to the final conclusions. But overall key individuals will feel a degree of ownership of the strategies, or at the least an understanding of why those particular strategies were chosen.

❏ Building knowledge of the business

In recognition of the importance of both building commitment and the quality of day-to-day decisions made by individual managers, emphasis needs to be placed on strategic planning as a learning process. Taking commitment first, it is in part built by understanding not only the strategies but also the reasoning behind the choice of those strategies. Unity of purpose can be served by sharing in the analysis of the external trends likely to affect an organisation's future. In the private sector, a shared realisation that a particular product is nearing saturation point, because nearly every family now has one, may be essential to mobilising effort to develop new products. In the public sector, shared understanding of the priorities of, for example, benefit recipients or applicants for passports, would help to build commitment to any changes in policy implied by those priorities. A shared realisation that pressure to hold down public expenditure is unlikely to ease may also be essential to building unity behind major efforts to improve efficiency or behind a search for alternative sources of funding, for example, for the arts.

The second aspect of planning as a learning process is that it can inform day-to-day decisions. The delivery of strategy depends on the multitude of decisions taken day by day by individual managers. If they have participated in the strategic planning process, understanding both the strategies and the reasoning behind them, their decisions will be better informed. Those managers will understand more about the environment in which they operate and about the outcomes required.

❏ Coherence

The earlier quotation from Bryson about top-down and bottom-up planning emphasised the need for detailed strategies, developed within the organisation, to be reviewed at the top for consistency. Strategy is not just a corporate matter. Each significant business unit needs its own strategy, fitting coherently within the strategy of the organisation as a whole. Smaller business units, or divisions, may not have strategies of their own, if by strategy is meant a plan covering a period of years. However, the objectives of any small unit, indeed of any individual, for a period as short as a few months, must be consistent with the strategic objectives at corporate level. For example, success for an organisation such as the Driving Standards Agency in meeting its strategic objectives will ultimately be dependent on the actions and behaviour of its driving test examiners. Planning cannot be confined to the top of an organisation, consistent sets of plans are required at and across all levels.

Achievement of purpose

Clarifying purpose and achieving unity of purpose will make success more likely without in themselves being sufficient. A planning process needs to go further to ensure that the chosen strategy can be delivered. This involves objective analysis of the feasibility of the preferred path, ensuring that the resources required are available, clarification of who is responsible for what, and setting up a basis for monitoring progress.

❏ Feasibility

In recent years a good deal of emphasis has been given to the need for top management to become fully involved in the planning process. There was a time when planning tended to be delegated largely to a planning department, staffed with highly intelligent staff with advanced computing skills. They would produce a plan, with detailed forecasts, showing optimal paths to business growth and profit, specifying the action required from each part of the business. This may be something of a caricature. There would be some consultation with key staff, and the plan would ultimately have to be approved by the chief executive and the Board. However, feelings of ownership of the plan probably rested more with the planning department than with the Board. Quite rightly there has, for some years now, been emphasis on ownership by top management, as in the case of ICI (Pink, 1988):

> 'The Executive Team are the Planners.' This is a statement made whenever a member of the Planning Department discusses Corporate Planning at ICI. The Chairman and Executive Directors exert clear strategic leadership on the ICI Group. The role of the Planning Department ... is to support the Executive Team in its strategic role and to facilitate the strategic dialogue between the Executive Team and the units through whom corporate strategy must largely be implemented.

This change in emphasis seems sometimes to have generated a different problem, with management teams moving to an opposite extreme. The author has been asked, on a number of occasions, to facilitate a strategic planning process consisting of little or nothing more than a two-day team meeting away from the office, the aim being to formulate a corporate strategy. The danger is twofold:

- there is a risk of failure to gain commitment widely across the organisation
- there is insufficient time (and information) to permit an objective analysis of the feasibility of the preferred strategy or strategies.

Planning is an opportunity to analyse carefully the purpose of the organisation, and to consider what strategies can actually deliver that purpose, given the possible trends and pressures in the external environment, the resources likely to be available, and the current capability of the organisation and the potential for changing it. It is an opportunity to stand back from the pressures of day-to-day management and consider carefully whether there are other ways of doing things which are more likely to bring success in the longer term. It is not simply about defining a purpose and uniting behind it, but also about identifying the means,

7

policies and initiatives capable of delivering it. If this is done well, the chances of establishing a reputation as a successful organisation are enhanced.

❏ Resourcing

One of the reasons why so much emphasis has been placed on written plans in central Government has been their role in supporting bids in the annual public expenditure survey. Non-departmental public bodies (NDPBs), executive agencies and nationalised industries have all been required to submit annual plans to their sponsoring Government departments, to inform those departments' own bids to and discussions with the Treasury. The bidding element is a legitimate integral part of the planning process in the private as well as the public sector. It is part of the merging of the top-down with the bottom-up.

Aims and objectives can only be met if the appropriate level of resources is available. Financial resources are of crucial importance, because they ultimately make it possible to employ staff and buy materials and equipment. However, finance is not sufficient in itself. Do staff have the right training, the right attitudes to their work? Are there systems to ensure that suppliers have the capacity to deliver the right quality of goods and materials as and when they are needed? Are information systems capable of delivering promptly and accurately the information which managers need? The planning process is an opportunity to consider such questions and achieve a match between the outputs required and the resources available. It is this match which is important, not the volume of resources in itself. Although it is more comfortable to choose the desired outputs and then obtain the resources to achieve them, the world is not like that in either the private or the public sector. Private companies find that the attitudes of banks and the stock market to their desires for funds often force them to trim their aspirations to fit the resources available. Similarly in the public sector the balance between outputs and resources may sometimes need to be struck by modifying desired outputs.

❏ Clarification of responsibilities

Where plans stipulate that something needs changing, they also need to make clear who will take responsibility for achieving the change. Frustration with planning has often arisen from the feeling that plans do not lead to action. This is one of the reasons for the growing popularity of the term 'strategic management' as opposed to 'strategic planning', as is explained in Chapter 2.

The planning process is an opportunity to decide what action should be taken, but it needs to go further than that and generate action plans. In the late 1970s

British Rail produced some well-regarded plans, containing ideas about how the financial fortunes of the industry could be improved. However, the financial deficits kept rising, and rapidly. Eventually the planning process was changed to put a major emphasis on the production of action plans, where each key element of change was accompanied by an action plan which named the manager responsible for achieving it. Following this there was a period when the finances of British Rail were significantly improved.

Clarification of responsibilities can go further than linking names with actions. One of the issues which may emerge in a planning process is that of organisational structure, and how different units relate to each other. Job descriptions and statements of roles and responsibilities emerging from plans can contribute significantly to the achievement of desired outcomes.

Framework for day-to-day decisions

One lesson learned by approaches to corporate planning in the 1950s and 1960s was that, however sophisticated the methods employed, forecasts of the future are unreliable. A second lesson was that large centralised planning systems are too inflexible to react quickly to seize new opportunities and counter threats and to allow business managers to respond to local circumstances. If there is uncertainty and if an organisation is large and perhaps geographically dispersed, those best placed to react sensibly to events are those nearest the action, not a central planning department. However, as the direction taken by the organisation will depend heavily on all of these individual decisions, it is important that the decisions should be mutually consistent. That is where the plan can help, by clarifying for individual managers the ultimate aims, values, strategies and objectives of the organisation and of its component parts. It thereby provides a framework for delegation and a framework within which managers can monitor progress and respond to unexpected events.

❑ Delegation

It has been recognised that, in the fast changing world, speed of reaction is vital. In the private sector those who react fastest gain competitive advantage, assuming, of course, that speed of decision is not at the expense of quality of decision. Speed of decision often requires significant delegation to managers, to avoid long, slow chains of consultation and authorisation. In the public sector, too, it has been recognised that many decisions are best taken by those nearest the action, for example those in a local Benefits Office, the person actually discussing a complaint with a customer, and so on. The planning process, by clarifying the ultimate destination and the values of the organisation, enables individual

9

decisions to be taken within a consistent framework. The more involvement which the individual decision makers have had with the planning process, the greater their knowledge and understanding are likely to be.

❏ Basis for monitoring

If you are travelling on a journey and need to know which way to turn at a junction which you are approaching, it is useful firstly to know your ultimate destination, secondly to have a map, and thirdly to know where you are on that map. The planning process should result in a clear view of the hoped for destination and in a map of the route. That route offers the milestones against which progress can be assessed. The information on progress against these milestones can then inform day-to-day decision making, helping managers to decide on and take corrective action wherever necessary.

❏ Responding to uncertainty

Keeping the same illustration, what happens if, during a journey, a road turns out unexpectedly to be blocked? A decision has to be taken, probably quickly, on how the previous plans should be changed. This is where it helps to have a clear idea of one's ultimate destination and of key points along the way. The ultimate destination offers guidance on the direction of travel and, once an unwelcome right hand turn has been necessary, suggests which turns are necessary to get back on course. The key points help because it may be possible to find signposts to these points if not to the ultimate destination.

Planning does not remove uncertainty, it helps people to understand it and live with it. Managers at all levels will be faced with the need to react to unexpected events. Their understanding of the ultimate destination, together with the business knowledge gained during the planning process, will help them to take those decisions, to take them quickly, to take them consistently, and to improve the chances of reaching the desired destination despite the hazards encountered en route.

Planning: a style of management

The purposes of planning described above are summarised in Figure 1.1. Looking at this summary, it is clear that planning should not be seen as an additional burden on managers who are already under stress. It is in fact integral to the responsibilities of managers. Planning is not an end in itself, it is an aid to management. It is hardly surprising that the Strategic Planning Society, in the United Kingdom, uses as its strapline:

> better management through planning.

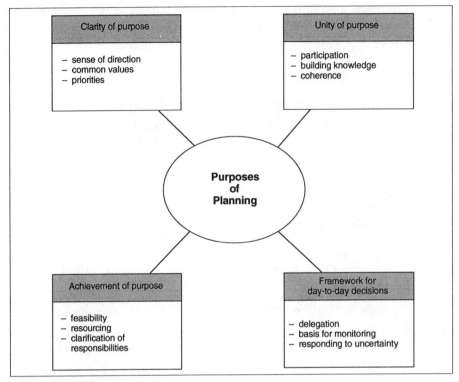

Figure 1.1. Purposes of planning.

At a strategic planning seminar, just a couple of years ago, one member of the audience asked two distinguished speakers from major companies:

> how much does your strategic planning process cost to run?

Neither speaker was able to offer an answer, somewhat to the aggravation of the questioner. Unfortunately there was no meeting of minds. To the speakers the question only made sense if put another way:

> how much would it cost not to have your strategic planning process?

The introduction of strategic planning should help to release senior management time rather than adding to the manager's load. It should provide clarity of direction and eliminate the need to revisit issues repeatedly. By checking feasibility and addressing resource issues, it should reduce the number of problems encountered. Through clarifying responsibilities and providing a framework for delegated decision making it should reduce the number of issues which senior managers personally have to address on a day-to-day basis. The author's own experience is that the introduction of planning into one recent post eventually freed approximately half of his time, which was then filled, hopefully productively, by taking on other responsibilities. This happened because, from the planning, individuals knew what was expected of them and were able to make their own decisions without constantly referring the issues upwards.

The main problem is that time is only freed when the planning process has matured. During the early stages the manager is required to undertake the planning while continuing to operate in the old style. That does amount to a considerable burden. These initial stages need a high level of dedication or some additional resources but, in the longer term, planning should become an integral part of the management process rather than an additional responsibility.

Where planning is an integral part of the management process, the signs are likely to be:

- managers at all levels are acquainted with the plan, and exhibit commitment to it
- everyone knows how their own responsibilities and objectives relate to the plan
- at all levels, the plan is recognised as the constant point of reference for assessing performance
- managers at all levels see the planning process as a help to them.

The process described in this book is designed to try to achieve those results.

References

Bryson, J. (1988) *Strategic Planning for Public and Nonprofit Organizations* London, Jossey-Bass

Pink, A. (1988) *Strategic Leadership through Corporate Planning at ICI* in *Long Range Planning* vol 21 No 1, Oxford, Pergamon Press

Johnson, G. and Scholes, K. (1984) *Exploring Corporate Strategy*
London, Prentice-Hall

Chapter 2

Strategic management: terminology and definitions

The literature of strategic management and planning is a terminological mine-field. Different organisations use the same terms to describe different things, or different terms to describe the same thing. So what are the differences, if any, between strategic management, strategic planning, corporate strategy, corporate planning, business strategy, business planning, action planning and management planning?

In Chapter 1 an important conclusion was that planning should be seen as a style of management, not as an additional burden placed on the manager. To reinforce that message, 'corporate planning', for many years the planning term in most common use in the public sector, was defined by the Civil Service College, as in Figure 2.1, to embrace action and the delivery of aspirations. Planning should not stop at the point where a vision of the future has emerged! It appears to be this same concern with the need for action which has led many writers in recent years to drop the term 'strategic planning' and to adopt instead the phrase 'strategic management'. Interestingly, the United Kingdom's Strategic Planning Society utilises the words strategic management rather than strategic planning in its mission, which is:

> to promote and communicate the understanding of effective strategic management and action.

The evolution of strategic management

The change in terminology from strategic planning to strategic management reflects changes in planning styles since the 1950s. The greatest concerns expressed about strategic planning can probably be summarised as follows:

- planning appeared to have become an end in itself, planning systems became centralised and bureaucratic, plans belonged to planners rather than to managers
- planning was done once a year, and when completed plans gathered dust on shelves

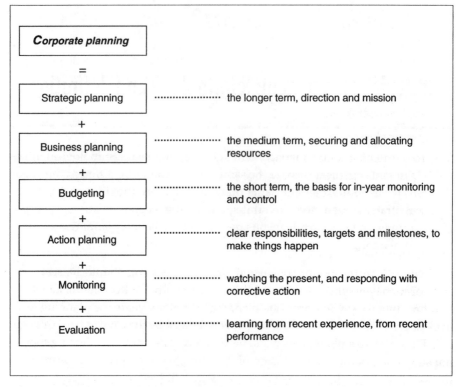

Figure 2.1. Corporate planning: a definition.

- plans tended to be overtaken by events, forecasts were inaccurate, strategies had to be changed, and original plans seemed a waste of time, having little influence on ultimate decisions
- centralised planning introduced inflexibility, obtaining authority to change anything could be a slow and cumbersome process
- planning still relied too much on extrapolation of the past and did not encourage radical thinking.

Greenley (1989) saw the evolution to strategic management as involving four stages:

- budgeting and control
- long range planning
- strategic planning
- strategic management.

Greenley's description of these stages is reproduced in Figure 2.2.

Budgeting and control

This represents early approaches to systematic management and is associated with the early years of the twentieth century. Based upon the assumption that past conditions will prevail in the future, the approach was simply to establish standard levels of performance in budgets and to compare these with actual levels. Reasons for any variations provided the only learning experiences.

Long-range planning

This is generally associated with the 1950s. The approach was based on the identification of past trends, particularly business growth, as well as methodology to project these trends into the future. Resources would then be planned either to exploit potential growth or to accommodate anticipated contraction.

Strategic planning

This is generally associated with the 1960s–70s. At this stage of development, past trends were considered to be inadequate, so that attention was focused on the total, albeit complex, market and business environment in which the firm participates. The focus was also placed upon identifying changes of direction, developing capabilities and creating strategic thrusts for competitive advantage. It was based on planning cycles, with the annual planning cycle being of particular importance.

Strategic management

This is associated with the period from the mid-1970s onwards. Like strategic planning, it is based on the complexities of the total business environment. However, the approach is not to accept current conditions as being restricting. Rather, the approach is led by well-defined aims, well-developed means to achieve them, and by pursuing viable opportunities wherever they can be identified, which may be regardless of the nature of current operations. The approach relies upon a continuous supply of information about the environment and avoids the use of planning cycles in preference to being based upon a continuous process.

Figure 2.2. Greenley's description of the historical development of strategic management.

Taylor and Harrison (1990) present a very similar history. They suggest the 1960s as the period of *long-range planning*, dominated by long-term forecasts, five-year budgets, detailed operational plans, and strategies for growth and diversification. Then, they suggest, the 1970s saw a change to *strategic planning*, with more emphasis on explicit company strategy, exploratory forecasting, simulations of alternative strategies, and planning for social and political change. This involved scenario planning, social forecasting and portfolio analysis amongst other techniques. The 1980s is then presented as the period of *strategic management*, with top management in charge of strategy, a total business approach of strategy formation and implementation, and emphasis on change management, visible leadership and staff involvement.

Different authors will present slightly different pictures of how planning styles have changed since the 1950s, but there are many common threads. Essentially there has been a move away from centralised, mathematical and deterministic systems through coordinated systems employing soft rather than hard analytical techniques, to flexible, delegated and supportive systems.

❏ Centralised systems

The centralised and deterministic systems can perhaps be caricatured as an attempt to concentrate many of the best brains in an organisation on forward planning, so as to reduce uncertainty by producing the best possible forecasts of the future and identifying the strategies best able to deliver corporate growth. This style was associated with:

- strong central control
- powerful planning teams
- planning processes and techniques poorly understood by line managers
- little effective participation by even relatively senior managers in strategic decision making.

Despite the brainpower employed, the attempts to forecast the future were far from a roaring success. Decision making processes were cumbersome, and many issues had to be resolved on a day-to-day basis by operational managers with little commitment to and little reference to the long-term plans.

❏ Co-ordinated systems

A key feature of co-ordinated systems is an attempt to merge top-down processes with an element of bottom-up planning, in recognition of:

- the need to involve managers to gain their commitment
- the benefits of exploiting the business knowledge of managers who are closer to the front line
- the impossibility of being deterministic about the future and the resulting need to leave some important decisions to individual managers.

The failure of the more mathematical techniques to produce successful forecasts of the future also encouraged the development of softer techniques, largely structured thinking processes. This allowed individual managers to participate in a way which was not possible when the techniques required an advanced qualification in mathematics, physics, economics or operational research!

Line managers might participate in the development of corporation-wide strategies, but they would certainly participate through the preparation of plans, to support those strategies, for their own commands. There would then be a series of coordinated and mutually consistent plans, and the role of the planning department would be to coordinate the process, to take a lead in ensuring consistency between plans, and to advise top managers on whether these plans delivered the desired *corporate* strategy.

❏ Delegated systems

There could be some debate as to whether the latest developments represent a change of kind or merely a continuation of previous trends. The pace of change continues to increase, competition is becoming more global, and it is vital for any organisation to be able to respond rapidly to new demands made upon it. Public sector organisations are experiencing the pressures of rapid change, just as the private sector is. Speed of response is more likely where individual managers are empowered to take decisions, including decisions with strategic implications. The balance in the planning process has changed, with more emphasis on the development of strategy at local level. The centre still coordinates the process, but the centre may well concentrate, though not exclusively, on strategies which will help and support those who ultimately deliver the service to the customer.

There are still some strategic decisions to be made at the centre. Which markets, products or service should the organisation concentrate on? Which major capital investments have priority? There may also be a desire to ensure a common standard of service for all customers wherever they are, particularly in the public sector. However, there is likely to be a good deal of emphasis at the centre on managing change, establishing the right culture, communications and information systems, staff development and leadership. The role of the planning department has changed to that of facilitator. Coordination is still required but the emphasis is on providing support to key managers, establishing a supportive framework to enable key managers to act to achieve results.

❏ Strategic management

The term strategic management has tended to become associated particularly with the third of these styles. Different writers will inevitably describe the elements of strategic management in slightly different ways. However, they normally tend to cover:

- analysing the environment
- making choices about direction
- implementation.

A study of the literature suggests that some key features of strategic management could be summarised as in Figure 2.3.

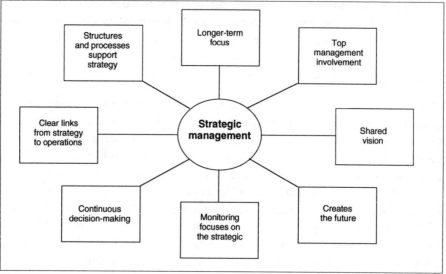

Figure 2.3. Features of strategic management.

Longer-term focus

A focus on the longer-term does not mean that no attention is paid to the present. On the contrary, there is emphasis on regular monitoring, but that monitoring should be designed to inform longer-term prospects and the results should be used to take action focused on improving the prospects of meeting longer-term objectives. Action plans, projects and budgets should flow from the strategy, they should not determine the strategy.

Top management involvement

Top management need to take the formulation of longer-term strategy seriously and should themselves play a major role in that process. They need to ensure that the organisation has an overall sense of direction, that they have consciously reviewed and determined objectives for the longer term, and that there are coherent strategies to meet those objectives. The analysis leading to those objectives and strategies should itself be recognised as objective, top management revealing a clear desire to understand and learn.

Shared vision

A shared vision implies:

- that conclusions are communicated to all those within the organisation who take decisions, probably everyone
- involvement in the planning process, both through consultation and through a proper mixture of top-down and bottom-up
- a strategy which is truly corporate, with meaning for everyone in the organisation.

Implementation of strategy depends upon actions taken by people throughout the organisation, so a wide understanding of critical factors is essential.

Creates the future

If the concern is with the longer term, strategies should not look simply like extrapolation of the past. Serious thought needs to be given to 'creating the future.' The strategy should therefore address thoroughly the scope of future activities and market choices. It should be sensitive to the underlying requirements of customers and to the wide constituency of stakeholders rather than loyal to what has always been done. There should be a strong element of the proactive.

Monitoring the strategic

Monitoring must be continuous, but it must also focus on the strategic. The relationship between the items monitored in-year and the longer-term objectives must be clear. Monitoring therefore needs to embrace items such as customer perceptions, underlying quality, efficiency and capability as well as immediate financial performance. The items monitored may include not only business results but developments in the external environment which do or could have major implications for the strategy.

Continuous decision-making

With strategic management the idea of continuous decision-making is emphasised, in contrast to the potentially stop–start decision-making process of an annual planning cycle. However, it is important to guard against continuous decision-making which degenerates into erratic decision-making. Within the overall direction of the strategy, or within the understanding developed during the strategy formulation process of the sensitivity of that strategy to the external environment, changes in course may be necessary. This is different from regular changes of mind, which would create confusion.

19

Clear links from strategy to operations

The underlying thought here is very close to that explained earlier in relation to monitoring. Action plans, projects and budgets should flow from the strategy, they should not effectively determine the strategy. The need for action plans, projects and budgets has to be stressed; long-term objectives and vision are not sufficient in themselves. People throughout the organisation need to know what is expected of them. In many cases individuals may be the prime movers in proposing or even deciding what they should do, in the light of the corporate objectives and vision. However, corporate management must ensure that the link to strategy is a strong one.

Structures and processes support strategy

If an organisation is set up on functional lines, is it capable of an effective customer orientation? Do management and communication processes ensure that strategic issues are rapidly shared and resolved, or do such issues tend to submerge and reappear? Is the strategy consistent with the culture of the organisation, the accepted norms of behaviour? Do personal reward, promotion and recruitment systems support and reinforce the qualities required in the longer term to deliver the strategy successfully?

Strategic management and planning

It has to be said that the features of strategic management listed above in effect compare it with non-strategic management rather than with strategic planning or corporate planning. Strategic management places a good deal of emphasis on forward planning but emphasises implementation as well. However, texts on strategic or corporate planning also often stress the need to develop action plans, to make sure that things happen. As in the example of Figure 2.1, they go on to see implementation processes as an integral part of planning. For example, Goodstein, Nolan and Pfeiffer (1992) write:

> Strategic planning is much more than just an envisioning process. It requires setting clear goals and objectives during specified periods in order to reach the planned future state.

Their book, entitled *Applied Strategic Planning*, takes the process from 'planning to plan', through steps such as environmental monitoring, mission formulation, modelling, performance audit, action planning and contingency planning, to 'implementation', which in turn embraces roles, structures, ownership of the plan, monitoring, and so on.

In conclusion, then, too much should not be made of terminological distinctions between 'strategic management', 'strategic planning' and 'corporate planning' and any associated phrases. For the purposes of this book we shall take strategic management as the all embracing term, equivalent to the use of the term 'corporate planning' in Figure 2.1. It is defined to cover the whole process from developing the long term vision to the implementation of decisions, the regular business monitoring of the results of those decisions, and ultimately to any necessary corrective action identified from the monitoring.

This means that 'strategic management' will embrace:

- strategic planning
- business planning
- budgeting
- monitoring
- evaluation
- action planning.

We shall now look at each of these elements in turn, before mentioning one or two other terms which tend to be used in the public sector.

❑ Strategic planning

Strategic planning concentrates on long-term purpose and direction, on the key issues which face the organisation in the longer term. First of all, what is meant by long term? Inevitably, the response is that 'it all depends'. To a company concerned about oil exploration, it may be necessary to think about potential developments up to fifty years ahead. To a railway operator investing in rolling stock which lasts thirty years and which has no alternative use, it will be important to think about the potential market over that sort of period. A ferry operator may be able to plan to a shorter horizon. Although new ships are expensive and have a long operating life, it may be possible to sell the asset to another operator in a different part of the world, in which case a planning horizon of, perhaps, ten years might be sufficient. Turning to central Government, the Ministry of Defence may need to plan on at least a ten-year horizon where procurement of major equipment is involved. In cases where the product is a service to the public, with little in the way of fixed assets without alternative uses, the horizon for a strategic plan could be shorter. Many public sector organisations do tend to come into this category and find that a five-year horizon is sufficient. Some use an even shorter horizon. An example has been the Lord Chancellor's Department, whose planning process is described in detail in

Chapter 12, but they are considering extending the period to five years. Ultimately the appropriate horizon depends on the nature of the strategic issues.

So what are strategic issues? They concern the basic direction, purpose, style and values of an organisation, and will embrace major projects, including large capital investments. Examples might include:

- decisions to concentrate on products which involve high technology
- changing the balance of the product or service mix or the product or service range
- breaking a company into separate parts, because it has grown too large to be managed effectively as a single entity
- setting up production facilities in a different part of the world to facilitate penetration of local markets
- major relocation of operations
- deciding that new technology will make it acceptable to close down all local offices
- changing organisational structure from one based on functions to one based on customer groupings or regions
- changes in pay and grading structures and performance management systems
- changing the mix of skills and experience of the staff
- establishing a set of core values or changing the internal culture of an organisation.

Most of these are just as applicable to the public sector as to the private sector. A number of executive agencies within Government have changed the range of services offered, for example the Vehicle Inspectorate. The Stationery Office has changed its pay and grading structures in a major way, and many other agencies are now required to develop their own structures. The National Health Service Management Executive has relocated from London to Leeds. The Driver and Vehicle Licensing Agency has decided to close down all its local offices. The Benefits Agency has established a set of core values.

One public sector organisation claimed that it could not develop a longer term strategy because it was demand led, it simply had to deal with cases when they came in and the flow of cases could not be predicted. It transpired that, if there were a rush of cases, the effect would be felt in two ways, a slower turn-round for the 'customer' and working of excess hours for the staff. In fact, this called out urgently for a new strategy, to build an organisation better capable of dealing with fluctuations in workload.

How frequently should a new strategic plan be prepared? Again, it depends on circumstances. A major unforeseen change in the environment could necessitate a new plan after six months or a year. Generally speaking, though, a strategic plan should remain valid for three years, or even four years in a stable environment. The strategy needs to be reviewed annually, the key assumptions need to be checked and the implications of any changes in those assumptions followed through. However, it should not need completely rewriting annually, at least not if it is a good strategy!

❏ Business plan

Planners at Shell have referred to their business plan as 'resourcing the strategy'. Once the basic direction has been decided, it is necessary to determine what the organisation will seek to achieve over the medium term to move in that direction. If the strategy says that the balance of the product mix should be changed, which specific products should be dropped or developed and when? If the management style needs to be changed, what specific initiatives should be pursued? What resources are likely to be available or could be obtained? What does this imply for the speed at which we can move along the strategic path which has been chosen? How should the resources obtained be allocated for the maximum contribution towards realising the strategy?

The business plan is the place where many difficult decisions have to be taken, in the attempt to reconcile immediate pressures with the longer-term strategy. It has a central place in the allocation of resources and would therefore normally be repeated at least annually. It focuses on the medium term, commonly around three years. Within the public sector, in the central Government sector at least, there is considerable advantage in a three-year horizon for the business plan because it fits with the three years covered by the public expenditure survey.

❏ The budget

The budget should form the basis of in-year monitoring and control. In the interests of strategic management, the business plan has to be compatible with the strategic plan, and the budget must be compatible with the business plan, otherwise monitoring will not be properly linked to the strategy. To this end, the budget should be identical to the first year of the business plan, but will probably need to be worked out in a bit more detail and cascaded right down through the organisation.

The mistake should not be made of thinking of a budget as covering only finance, only receipts and expenditure. The term as used here embraces the outputs required, levels of efficiency (linking outputs to inputs), and the milestones which need to be reached if the medium-term goals are to be achieved. A budget would be expected to look one year ahead, to be produced at least annually, and to be reviewed on a regular basis throughout the year.

❑ Monitoring

Monitoring is an in-year activity, basically comparing performance with the budget. If the budget is year one of the business plan, monitoring against the budget amounts to monitoring against the business plan. Thinking in terms of a journey, the plan starts with the ultimate destination. The 'budget' would show where we need to be at a particular point in time. Monitoring our progress shows where we actually are, we then compare that with where we wanted to be, and decide what action to take as a result. This could involve speeding up, realising that we can afford to take in an additional stop, trying a different route, or even, in extremes, deciding that the journey is not feasible and choosing a different destination. Or, if we are where we ought to be, the decision could be simply to continue as planned.

The important things are that:

- monitoring should be planned in to the plan, the targets and milestones should be set, and information systems set up to allow progress to be checked
- monitoring is taken seriously, and the implications of the monitoring results are considered objectively.

❑ Evaluation

Evaluation is primarily an end of year activity. How has performance turned out, compared with what we were hoping for? Where did things go wrong and why? Where did they go well and why? When these questions have been answered, the next step is to consider the implications for the business plan and the strategy. Are the targets in those plans still feasible? Are the problems so severe that a completely new strategy is required? Or is the strategy still valid but we need to take drastic action in the business plan to retrieve the situation? Alternatively, have the results been so good that we ought to be setting ourselves some more demanding targets in the business plan?

❑ Action planning

The five elements considered above, strategic planning, business planning, budgeting, monitoring and evaluation, are in some senses sequential. One tends to follow the other chronologically, though clearly the messages from monitoring and evaluation feed back into future business plans and budgets, while the preparation of business plans and budgets can lead to modifications to the strategy. Elements of action planning are required at all stages, however. Action planning is implicit in the use of terms such as 'identifying specific goals to be achieved' or 'identifying the milestones'. It is important that planning and budgeting processes should go further than setting the goals and milestones:

- firstly, it is essential to identify who will have lead responsibility for achieving the goals and milestones
- secondly, each individual will need to clarify the actions which will enable him or her to meet them.

At the level of the strategic plan, it is unlikely that there will be a requirement for detailed action plans. In the case of some major initiatives, particularly major capital projects, there may need to be quite detailed checks of feasibility and viability. In other cases, action planning at the strategic level may take the form of a somewhat broader validation, a check that people can identify initiatives which would reliably take the organisation in the desired direction. When it comes to business plans and budgets, individuals responsible for particular goals will need their own detailed action plans, often in the form of project plans. Although these individuals must 'own' the plans, in the case of major initiatives with an organisation-wide impact senior managers are likely to wish to ensure personally:

- that action plans do exist
- that they appear likely to be capable of delivering the end result required.

❑ Other terms

In the preceding paragraphs definitions have been offered of strategic plans, business plans and budgets. These definitions are the ones which will be implied wherever these terms are used subsequently in this book. However, it should be emphasised that the concepts lying behind the definitions are the important things, not the actual terminology. Others may use the terms in different ways and that is perfectly acceptable. There are also some other terms which are in common usage. Two of these which are particularly common in the public sector are corporate plans and management plans.

Corporate plans

It is very common for three-year plans produced by non-departmental public bodies and by executive agencies to be referred to as corporate plans. Some time ago there was a lot of emphasis on the need for nationalised industries and non-departmental public bodies to produce 'corporate plans', to inform the public expenditure survey and to form a focal point for their relationship with their sponsoring departments. The role of these plans was very much that embraced by the definition of business plans earlier.

The term ' corporate plan' is also sometimes used to refer to the plan produced for an organisation as a whole, for the corporate entity. This plan is distinguished from 'business plans' which are the plans for individual business units, or subsidiaries, or divisions. This distinction between plans for the corporate body and plans for individual units could apply equally to long-term or to medium-term plans. In the case of long-term plans there may then be both 'corporate strategy' and 'business strategy.'

Management plans

The term 'management plan' is sometimes used to refer to the one-year plan which we have called the 'budget'. In this usage it may be distinguished from a budget, which would then cover only the financial aspects. There are also instances of the term 'management plan' being used to refer to the three-year plan which we have called a 'business plan.'

There is also another specialised use sometimes made of the term 'management plan' in the central Government sector. Within the public expenditure control system there is a specific control, for each Government department, on the level of running costs, the costs of departmental administration. Each department has been required to submit running cost management plans to the Treasury, as a basis for discussion of what level of running costs should be agreed. There are therefore cases where the term 'management plan' may be used specifically to refer to a plan concentrating on the costs of departmental administration.

References

Goodstein, L. D. Nolan, T. M. and Pfeiffer, J. W. (1992) *Applied Strategic Planning: A Comprehensive Guide* San Diego, Pfeiffer and Company

Greenley, G. E. (1989) *Strategic Management* Hemel Hempstead, Prentice-Hall

Taylor, B. and Harrison, J. (1990) *The Manager's Casebook of Business Strategy* Oxford, Butterworth Heinemann

Chapter 3

The components of strategic management

The strategic management process is not a simple, sequential, set chain of activities, though, in a book, it often ends up appearing that way. In any individual organisation the process needs to be adapted to address that organisation's particular circumstances. The models presented here are therefore just that, models. Hopefully they provide insight, but the insight then has to be used to choose the right way to proceed in an individual situation. The models cannot be prescriptive.

In essence there are three key stages in the strategic management or planning process, which are referred to at the Civil Service College as the three As, illustrated in Figure 3.1.

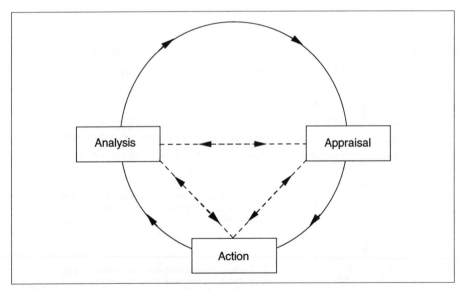

Figure 3.1. Strategic management: the three As.

To the extent that there is a chronological sequence (the unbroken line) the starting point is analysis, followed by appraisal of options, followed by action. Experience of action then feeds back into the analysis stage for the next planning cycle. However, it is often found that when options are being considered there may be reason to go back and query some of the analytical work. Or attempts to prepare action plans may raise questions about the analysis or about the consideration of options. Hence the dotted lines in the Figure.

Each stage, each of the three As, will now be considered in turn and broken down into a number of separate components which will be described in more detail. The three As apply whether one is referring to the annual cycle associated with business plans or the less frequent cycle associated with strategic plans. However, the emphasis placed on particular components within the stages is likely to differ between the two cycles. The possible differences in emphasis will be explained as we go along.

Analysis

The analysis stage is itself broken down into six elements as illustrated in Figure 3.2. Each component will be considered in turn.

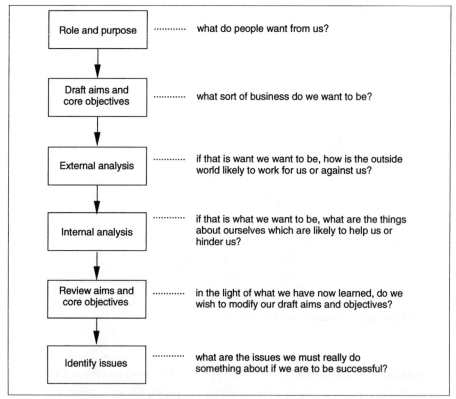

Figure 3.2. The components of the analysis stage.

❏ Role and purpose

This component of the planning process is likely to take much greater prominence for a public sector organisation than for a private sector organisation. This is not to deny that in the private sector companies need to decide which business they are in. For example, some passenger shipping lines had to decide whether they were really in the transport business or the hotel business; the choice had significant implications for both the facilities offered and the style of marketing. Private companies, however, have a good deal of freedom, at the corporate level, to choose their own business, as long as the shareholders are content that the chosen course does not endanger their funds. An individual business unit will be more constrained, however, and will need to work within guidelines laid down by the corporate strategy.

There was a time when it was said that in the private sector you could do anything which was not forbidden by law whereas in the public sector you could do only what was expressly permitted by law. The distinction is not as clear cut as this statement implies, but the author has certainly been involved with issues in the nationalised industries, both railways and water, where considerable time had to be spent checking legislation to see if it permitted some minor element of diversification which the industries had proposed. It remains true that careful thought needs to be given by any public sector organisation to what it is required to do, what it is permitted to do, what it is expected to do and the boundaries between them.

Two techniques which can be used to help to identify role and purpose are:

- mandates analysis
- stakeholder analysis.

Each of these will be explained in Chapter 4.

It should be clear that the role and purpose of an organisation ought not to change very frequently. Therefore, while a full mandates and stakeholder analysis should be undertaken during the preparation of a strategic plan, it does not need to be repeated in the annual business planning cycle. The analysis should be reviewed annually, to consider whether anything has, or might have, changed, and the implications of any change need to be incorporated into the business plan. If the change is significant, however, it probably implies a need for a new strategic plan!

❏ Draft aims and core objectives

The draft aims and core objectives in effect sum up the key conclusions of the mandates and stakeholder analyses. They summarise what the key interests would expect the organisation to seek to be. As will be seen when we look at stakeholder analysis, the key interests are not all outsiders. There is scope for the management and staff of the organisation to influence the thinking behind the aims and core objectives. However, most public sector organisations are ultimately accountable to Government ministers, through those ministers to Parliament, and to the public as taxpayer and sometimes direct recipient of the service. The requirements of these people will therefore exert strong influence on the choice of aims and core objectives.

The word 'aims' has been used where others might choose to use the word 'mission' or even 'purpose' or 'role'. What is meant here is a short statement, probably no more than one sentence, which sums up what the organisation should seek to be. The 'core objectives' will break that down into more specific elements, but will continue to reflect the underlying purpose. The term 'core objectives' is used to contrast with 'change objectives' which will emerge from later stages of the planning process. 'Core objectives' are likely to remain applicable, with no more than minor modifications, for many years, whereas 'change objectives' will reflect initiatives which are likely to have a completion date.

Writers on strategy sometimes differ in their view of where the formulation of aims and core objectives appears in the strategic planning process. Some writers take the view that aims and core objectives are either given or formulated right at the start. Strategic planning then concentrates on identifying strategies to enable the organisation to achieve those aims and objectives. The view taken here is that aims and core objectives are an output from the strategic plan. It is recognised that some view of purpose is needed at an early stage to inform the analysis. For example, it is difficult to decide what is a current strength and what is a weakness without some idea of the end result required. To reflect this, *draft* aims and core objectives are proposed immediately after the analysis of mandates and stakeholders but are then revisited from time to time and not finalised until the late stages of the planning.

Just as the role and purpose of an organisation is not likely to change annually, the aims and core objectives, by definition, will retain their currency for a number of years. While they should be reviewed annually in the business planning cycle, they should only normally require reformulating every few years in the strategic planning cycle.

❏ External analysis

Will the outside world be working in our favour or against us? Will the demand for the service we provide be rising or falling? Will the economy make it increasingly difficult for us to obtain the resources we require? Are social and political pressures likely to result in attitudes or legislation which threaten our current approach or even our existence? Are there alternative providers of the service or even alternative services which could reduce the need for us? These are the types of questions which need to be addressed during the external analysis.

A range of techniques is available to help with this component of the planning process. Those described in Chapter 5 are:

- PEST
- forecasting models (time series and econometric models)
- market research
- focus groups
- delphi
- scenarios.

❑ Internal analysis

The distinction between internal and external analysis is not necessarily a clear and rigid one. In theory it is useful to separate them, primarily to check that both external and internal elements have been adequately covered. In practice, though, many techniques tend to cross the boundaries. Those which most obviously cross the boundaries are considered in the next section, identification of issues.

The emphasis in the internal analysis is on identifying where performance is strong or weak. This means looking at performance relative to the expectations of customers and other stakeholders and relative to the performance of other organisations. It also means looking at questions of internal structure, attitudes, values, culture, skills and capabilities. Some of the techniques which can be used to help with the internal analysis are described in Chapter 6:

- benchmarking
- the Boston portfolio matrix
- product life cycles
- value chain analysis
- the 7–S framework.

Focus groups, described under the heading of external analysis, can be helpful for internal analysis as well. Most of the techniques mentioned here and in the previous section are not intended for use every year. They would therefore be more appropriate to a strategic planning than to a business planning cycle. There will be occasions when particular analyses need to be reviewed between strategic plans. Generally, though, in the business planning cycle the external and internal analysis will concentrate on examining the recent outturn against what had been planned and establishing the reasons for the variances. This would identify:

- where particular elements of the strategy need to be speeded up or slowed down

- where some new initiative is needed in response to a particular external event to bring us back on track

- where an element of the strategy needs to be revisited.

In either of the second or third cases some of the specific techniques listed above might prove helpful.

❏ Review aims and core objectives

Once both the external and the internal analysis have been completed, the draft aims and core objectives should be revisited, to check that nothing at this stage has suggested any modification to them. Remember, though, that it is only the core objectives, describing the organisation's basic purpose, which are being reviewed. There is no need yet to draft any change objectives, although some might by now be emerging quite clearly. For example, if a major problem identified is high overheads it is pretty clear that an important objective will be to reduce them. That is a change objective; however, it is not the basic purpose of the organisation, it is something which needs to be done in order to achieve that basic purpose, or to achieve it better.

Is it really possible for the view of aims and core objectives to change significantly at this point? The additional information gathered on likely political and economic developments might suggest that some of the objectives originally drafted might not really be sustainable in five years' time. For example, it might be felt that the public funding required is most unlikely to be available. Or perhaps the information gathered on potential competitors may suggest that a specific reference to the competitive position would be helpful. Maybe it now appears that the emphasis on service quality is likely to be stronger than we had first assumed. This could even be the moment when, having looked at the competition and market trends, you decide that you should be in the transport business rather than the railway business, or in the utilities business rather than the electricity business, or in the pharmaceutical rather than the fertiliser business. Such a significant change may be rare, but some time should be set aside for objective review to check, because any change could have a major influence on the selection of key issues.

❏ Identification of issues

The final element of the analysis stage is the identification of issues, perhaps better defined as the key issues, or, in the case of strategic planning, the strategic issues. As defined in Figure 3.2, these are the issues which we must do something about if we are to be successful. Sometimes people may use the term key success factors or critical success factors. These are related to the key issues. Putting a key issue right can be thought of as a key success factor.

Some issues may emerge directly from the external analysis, some from the internal analysis. However, the most important, most strategic issues may well emerge from putting the internal and external analysis together. There are some techniques which do themselves span both the internal and external situation. Examples described later in Chapter 7 are:

- portfolio models
- gap analysis
- competitive advantage.

One approach which is virtually indispensable as a way of helping to bring all of the analysis together is a *SWOT* analysis, a listing of strengths, weaknesses, opportunities and threats. This too is described in Chapter 7.

Again it is unlikely that the techniques mentioned here will need to be applied every year in the business planning cycle. The issues in business planning are most likely to emerge as a failure to meet some specific targets or as a change in one or more key assumptions about the external environment.

Appraisal

The second stage of the planning process involves the examination of the options available. It can be broken down into the four components shown in Figure 3.3.

The whole of the appraisal stage applies equally to both the strategic planning and the business planning cycles. In both cases a set of issues will have been derived, and choices arising from these issues will have to be made.

❏ Categorisation of issues

Each of the issues needs to be addressed, but the nature and extent of the appraisal necessary can differ considerably between issues. Broadly, issues can be divided into three categories:

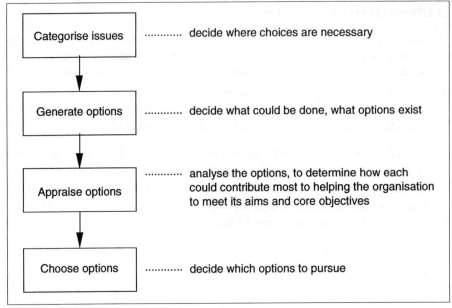

Figure 3.3. The components of the appraisal stage.

- those where there are major choices as to both the implied objective and the courses of action
- those where the implied objective is clear but there are doubts as to which would be the best course of action to deliver that objective
- those where both the implied objective and the course of action required are clear.

All three might be illustrated by reference to a single issue, the range of services offered.

The first of the three categories would arise if it were not clear whether the organisation should seek to provide a wider range of services or should concentrate on a narrower range. This could well be an issue, for example, in research laboratories. The issue also arises in central Government departments, where there could be a need for major policy decisions on, say, the range of social security benefits or the services offered by the National Health Service.

The second category would arise where, from the analysis undertaken, it is clear that a wider range of services needs to be offered but where it is unclear which particular additional services would offer the greatest benefit. The third category implies a situation where the analysis stage has identified one specific gap in the services offered which needs to be filled.

Consider the case where the analysis has revealed a problem with the buildings which an organisation occupies. The position at the end of the analysis stage could fall into one of the three categories listed above:

- should we relocate, rebuild where we are, refurbish, or make do and mend
- we clearly need to refurbish, but which blocks take priority, or, we clearly need more office space but should it be a new block, a temporary building or a rented block somewhere in the locality
- we clearly need to refurbish one specific block.

The three categories are not mutually exclusive. It may be that an organisation needs to consider at one and the same time whether it should offer additional services and what they should be. For example, the Vehicle Inspectorate could be in that situation when deciding whether to offer vehicle tests in the evenings or at the weekends or an advisory service or whatever. If there is an issue with the buildings, the position may be that we need to consider at the same time whether we should relocate, rebuild, refurbish or make do and mend and, within each of these options, what the priorities should be.

The purpose of this work on categorising issues is to identify the scope and extent of the appraisal work necessary. Doing this carefully helps:

- to establish the importance of the appraisal stage, which is where key strategic decisions are made but where analysis is often skimped
- to set up a proper work programme to ensure that the choices are addressed systematically and objectively.

❏ Generating options

The danger at this point in the planning process is that people do not think radically enough about the possibilities available. There is often a tendency to concentrate on marginal change, work a bit faster, do a bit more of what we are already doing, tighten up a bit more on overheads, and so on. The need to consider radical alternatives to what is currently done is obviously particularly important in the strategic planning cycle, but there is also a need for radical thinking in business planning. When, at the analysis stage, it emerges that performance in a particular area of activity has been weak, how ready are people to acknowledge that the present approach is not working and that something completely different should be tried? Or is the more common reaction just to say that we must work harder at the current approach?

In central Government, every executive agency has to be reviewed every five years, in what is known as a 'prior options' exercise. The specification of this exercise requires people to consider radical alternatives to continuation as an executive agency of Government, alternatives such as:

- whether the work needs to be done at all
- whether it could be privatised
- whether it could be contracted out.

In this case, radical thinking is imposed by an external authority. When an organisation is planning its own future, equally radical thinking about what it needs to do and how it should do it is necessary. In Chapter 8, some approaches to releasing creativity to generate radical options are introduced, for example, brainstorming and fishboning. Emphasis is also placed on involving a wide range of people, to increase the volume and variety of ideas.

❏ Appraising options

The next component of the appraisal stage is weighing up the pros and cons of the options identified for consideration. Expanding on the explanatory words in Figure 3.3, this can perhaps be best summed up as:

> which options contribute most to our aims, building on our strengths, addressing our weaknesses, seizing our opportunities and countering the threats which face us?

That wording is rather general, perhaps the cue for a general discussion of the options to reach at best a consensus, at worst a compromise. There is danger here. Individuals often start with very clear ideas of which option they prefer, but these ideas may be based heavily on a particular experience or on a particular individual set of values. Ask honestly, when we see option appraisals how often are those appraisals designed to help people to find an answer, how often are they designed to justify to others a decision which has been taken on a quite different basis? There is a serious danger that senior management at this point will seek to interpret the facts to back what they feel they would like rather than seek objective, including unpleasant, information to help them to make the right decisions to achieve the ultimate aims of the organisation.

In Chapter 8 there is a section explaining techniques which can be used to structure the analysis to make it as helpful and objective as possible for decision makers. The principal techniques described are:

- discounted cash flow analysis (DCF)
- weighting and ranking.

The first of these techniques is essential wherever there is a significant financial dimension to the decisions. The Treasury would always expect a proper DCF analysis of any major capital project. 'Weighting and ranking' is likely to play a more important part in strategy formulation, particularly in the public sector. It is basically a structured thinking process, which involves identifying the key criteria for choosing between options, then marking each option against each criterion. Both hard factors (such as how much it costs), and soft factors (how well does it fit our values), can be considered together. In the public sector, soft factors, under the general heading of public and political acceptability, can play a very important part.

❏ Choosing options

In the light of the analysis and information now available, the time has come to decide which options to pursue. These decisions can take a variety of forms:

- particular capital projects eg relocation of headquarters, or a major piece of laboratory equipment
- clarification of basic direction eg which areas of activity should grow, which decline, how much growth should be sought overall
- individual studies or reviews to be undertaken eg areas for market testing, a new marketing strategy
- major initiatives, eg a new performance appraisal system, recruiting a new range of skills, introducing a new service.

The above examples are most likely to arise in the strategic planning cycle. In the business planning cycle there will probably be more emphasis on speeding things up or slowing things down, on financial decisions, on the details of capital projects including starting dates, on which reviews should be undertaken first and when they should be completed. The nature of the options in the strategic plan is likely to differ from the options in the business plan. They will by definition tend to be more strategic. However, the techniques for appraisal are the same in both cases.

Action

The final stage of the strategic management process is the action stage, making sure that things happen. This stage is broken down into the seven components shown in Figure 3.4. It will be seen that there is a great deal of emphasis on objectives rather than on detailed action plans. This may be a bit surprising, but it reflects the emphasis in management today on delegation and empowerment.

The thrust is on clarifying what people are expected to achieve, on the outputs and outcomes required, and then people are left with a good deal of freedom, (within boundaries of legality, financial authority and organisational values and style), to decide *how* to achieve it. Detailed action plans are still required, but they are largely for the individual to determine for himself or herself. Control is exerted through accountability for end results rather than through checking day-to-day activity. It should be said, though, that objectives and action plans can look very similar in the case of projects. The targets there will very often be in the form of milestones, whether particular actions have been completed by a particular date, and this is very similar to monitoring against action plans.

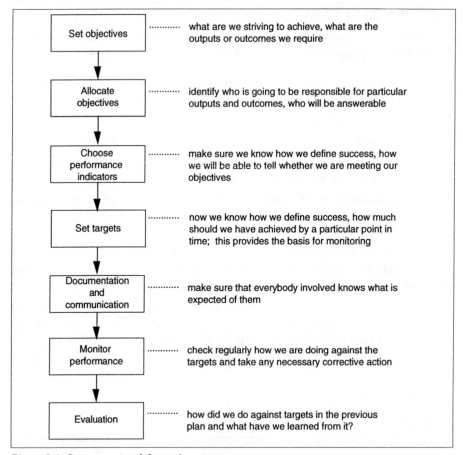

Figure 3.4. Components of the action stage.

❏ Setting and allocating objectives and targets

There is a risk in relying upon objectives rather than action plans as the basis for ensuring that things happen if the objectives themselves are not clear. Specifying clear objectives is often thought to be a particular problem in the public sector, because the demands made upon public sector organisations are complex. There has been a feeling that things are somewhat easier in the private sector, with its strong emphasis on financial results. Recent experiences of the private sector suggest that this is an over-simplification. Success is seen to depend upon many 'soft' factors, such as customer perceptions of service, attitudes of staff, image and so on. Large private sector companies have, in the last year or two, been joining together to share their experience of setting objectives for and choosing indicators for these more difficult but vital areas of performance.

In Chapter 9 some guidance is offered on the form which objectives should take if they are to be the basis for ensuring action. This is followed by some guide-lines on how to choose performance indicators and some thoughts on setting target values for the indicators.

One of the most important aspects of setting objectives is that the objectives for different people and different groups within the organisation fit together. They need to be:

- mutually consistent
- mutually supportive.

The second point means that, if all individuals and groups within an organisa-tion meet their objectives, the organisation as a whole will meet its objectives. Chapter 9 presents the Sunningdale model which is designed to ensure that these requirements are met.

How far is it necessary to go in ensuring a consistent set of objectives right through the organisation? In the case of budgets, looking one year ahead, every indi-vidual forward job plan plays its part in ensuring that corporate objectives are delivered. In the case of a strategic plan looking five years or more ahead, it may be felt sufficient to determine objectives only at the corporate level or perhaps to one management level below. Business plans, looking around three years ahead, fit between these two extremes. The appropriate time horizon for objectives at any level within an organisation needs to be judged by management in the light of the particular circumstances of that organisation.

Increasingly, modern organisations are finding that implementation requires projects which run across the traditional hierarchical command structures. The appraisal of some strategic issues may lead to a conclusion that particular tech-niques need to be applied to achieve major change. One approach which has been popular over recent years has been Total Quality Management. An approach enjoying much support at present is Business Process Re-engineering. Both of these are described briefly in Chapter 9.

❏ Documentation and communication

As will be clear from subsequent chapters, many people throughout the organisation should have been involved in the planning processes and should therefore have some understanding of the issues and the choices being made. However, when final decisions have been made it is important to ensure that these decisions are clearly understood and that everyone understands what is required of them personally.

A point to emphasise here is that documentation should be seen as an integral part of the planning process. It is neither the ultimate end-product nor the key element. Its role is to communicate. In the public sector there has been a tendency to see the production of a written 'corporate plan' as the ultimate objective, the primary purpose of the planning process. The quotation from a Treasury paper at the end of Chapter 1 emphasises the importance of the planning process itself.

In Chapter 10 we look at documentation in the context of requirements to communicate the decisions taken as a result of the planning process and consider what form the documentation might take for different audiences. Methods of communication other than written documentation are also briefly considered.

❏ Monitoring

Monitoring is an in-year activity, comparing performance with targets and identifying reasons why performance may be deviating from the targets. The Sunningdale model, mentioned earlier in the section on setting and allocating objectives and targets, offers a framework for monitoring. This is discussed in Chapter 9.

❏ Evaluation

Evaluation is listed in Figure 3.4 as the final component of the planning process. It involves looking back, analysing performance against targets in the previous plan, considering the implications and drawing lessons. Actually this stage serves little purpose except in so far as it is regarded as an element of the analysis stage for the next plan. Although evaluation looks at past data, its importance is the application of lessons learned to the future. As emphasised at the beginning of this chapter the planning process does not have a clear beginning and a clear end, it is rather a continuous process. The evaluation process is both the ending of one planning cycle and the beginning of the next.

Chapter 4

Aims and core objectives

This chapter concentrates on the first two components of the analysis stage of the strategic management process, the stage described in Figure 3.2. As explained in Chapter 3 there are two techniques which are helpful in establishing an organisation's basic role and purpose, namely:

- mandates analysis
- stakeholder analysis.

Each of these will be examined in turn, and the chapter will conclude with some thoughts about the formulation of the draft aims and core objectives which should be the outcome of the analysis.

Mandates analysis

'Mandates' is a word unlikely to be found in texts whose focus is the private sector, presumably because companies are free to choose which activities to undertake within the bounds of legality. A manager of an individual Business Unit within a company may feel less free, being bound to operate within an overall corporate strategy, but at corporate level businesses are free to diversify into or to withdraw from particular activities.

The situation in the public sector is quite different. Non-departmental public bodies may be governed by statutes which stipulate certain duties, activities which they must undertake. Government departments will have some duties which are embodied in legislation, as will some executive agencies. Every executive agency will have a framework document which stipulates some duties as well as setting out objectives, delegations and certain administrative arrangements which must be followed.

The purpose of the mandates analysis is to clarify the boundaries between:

- what must be done
- what could be done
- what must not be done.

The focus is on the requirements of those who hold some formal authority over the public sector body in question.

Establishing the minimum of what must be done is usually relatively straightforward. Look at any relevant legislation, look at a framework document, look at any formal correspondence from a Government minister or other person in authority. The mistake which is often made is to assume that this minimum is all that is permitted. Certainly legislation can be restrictive, and in some cases one has to work on the basis that a public sector body can only undertake activities which are specifically permitted by the legislation. For example, there have been major questions in the past about whether British Rail had the power to run substitute bus services and whether Water Authorities, when still public sector bodies, were allowed to diversify into activities such as the provision of consultancy services relating to civil engineering projects. However, there is a danger of treating legislation too restrictively. It often stipulates an activity, but it says little or nothing about the level of service to be offered to the public. For example, legislation could specify a requirement to provide driving tests and to recover costs, but without specifying a uniform level of service at a standard cost to everybody!

The Driving Standards Agency and others have shown that mandates are not so restrictive as to rule out consideration of enhanced services to the public. The Vehicle Inspectorate was free to introduce tests on Saturdays. Customers were willing to meet the extra cost of weekend working. It was a service which benefited them by enabling them to maximise productive use of their vehicles in the busy part of the week. There are many more examples of agencies realising that they are free to offer enhanced services to the public, whether it is selling special vehicle number plates, ordnance survey maps centred on a person's own home, or special editions of coins. As Bryson (1988) points out:

> Clarification of what is not ruled out is particularly important. Alerting organizational members to what they *might* do can lead to valuable discussions about what the organization's mission ought to be. Too many organizations think they are more constrained than they actually are and, indeed, make the fundamental error of assuming that their mandates and mission are the same. They may be, but planners should not start out with that assumption.

If stipulating the minimum of what is permitted is relatively straightforward, how should one go about establishing the boundary between what could be done and what must not be done? The first thing to say is that there is little point in attempting to produce long lists of what must not be done. The list could be endless and filled with items of no practical significance. A better approach is to try to identify activities which might be regarded as natural extensions of the current ones, in effect identify activities which to a private sector organisation would be natural candidates for diversification. Such a list relating to public libraries is given in Figure 4.1.

County Library Mandates analysis	Must	Could	Must not
Adult fiction	☐	☐	☐
Adult non-fiction	☐	☐	☐
Children's books	☐	☐	☐
Reference books	☐	☐	☐
Maps for reference	☐	☐	☐
Maps for loan	☐	☐	☐
Video recordings for loan	☐	☐	☐
Works of art for loan	☐	☐	☐
Special exhibitions relating to literature	☐	☐	☐
Special exhibitions not relating to literature	☐	☐	☐
Music concerts in library	☐	☐	☐
Arranging music concerts in other venues	☐	☐	☐
Opening on Sundays	☐	☐	☐
Advertising library services on television	☐	☐	☐
Contracting out the library service	☐	☐	☐
Close all but the central library	☐	☐	☐
Coffee shop in High Street	☐	☐	☐
Selling surplus books	☐	☐	☐
Selling new books in library	☐	☐	☐
Bookshop in High Street	☐	☐	☐

Please ✓ appropriate box

Figure 4.1. Mandates analysis for a public library.

In the case of the public library it was necessary to ask not only whether the service was in the category of 'must', 'could', or 'must not', but also whether the service had to be free, had to be charged for, or could be either. What was very revealing was the level of disagreement amongst a group of librarians from different parts of the country as to where the boundaries fell. Some argued that a particular service would never be permitted, only to discover that others were already providing it!

One of the reasons for disagreement is that mandates can be formal or informal. The formal ones, embodied in legislation, framework documents or instructions from those in authority, tend to be clear. They are mostly the positive mandates, the 'musts.' Informal mandates come into the category:

> there is nothing formally to stop us doing it, but if we did it there soon would be.

So, for example, it may be accepted that a public sector organisation can use surplus capacity to provide services in competition with the private sector, but the same organisation may feel that it would be unacceptable positively to build capacity to provide such services. There is inevitably scope for exercising a degree of judgement as to exactly where the boundaries lie.

At the end of the day, what are the main benefits of undertaking a mandates analysis? We suggest three main benefits:

- it identifies things which must be done, so that they can be incorporated clearly into the aims and core objectives, increasing the certainty that the organisation's basic purpose will be met
- at the same time, it helps to avoid expressing the aims and objectives so narrowly as to rule out possible developments which later analysis might suggest to be beneficial
- to use some management speak, it may help to 'change mind-sets', to get people thinking more freely about new possibilities and wider options.

Stakeholder analysis

Stakeholder analysis is a common feature of strategic management or planning in both the public and private sectors. It has become recognised that, although a private sector company may be thought of as having a prime responsibility to its shareholders, there are many others who have a 'stake' in the strategies of the company, for example employees and the local community. Argenti (1993) has described stakeholder theory as:

> a curse that lies heavily upon all our organisations.

However, his concern is with the ethics of the claims of groups classed as stakeholders to a 'stake' or share in the success of the company. He takes the view that recognition of a wide range of stakeholders can detract from the attention which should be given to prime interests. In the private sector that could be the shareholder, but in a school it should be the pupil. Thinking about the interests of the community, the teachers, local industry and so on may be to the detriment of the interests of that pupil. There is plenty of mileage yet in debate about the ethics of stakeholder analysis, but here we take an essentially pragmatic view. If someone has power and the potential to influence our success, it is better to recognise that power and its implications. That way there is a far better chance of ultimate success.

❑ Definition of stakeholders

A pragmatic definition of stakeholders is offered by Goodstein, Nolan and Pfeiffer (1992):

> those individuals, groups, and organizations who will be impacted by or who are likely to be interested in the organization's strategic plan and the planning process. Included are all who believe, rightly or wrongly, that they have a stake in the organization's future and not merely those whom the planning team believes have a reasonable or legitimate right to such a stake.

The approach to stakeholder analysis adopted here implies that we should treat as stakeholders any individual, any formal or informal grouping of individuals, or any institution which both wishes to and is able to affect our organisation's future. The power to affect public sector organisations can probably be split broadly into four categories:

- direct power over resources, usually associated with the formal power to issue directions stemming from a hierarchical relationship
- power of political influence, basically an indirect power over resources arising from the ability to influence those who have direct power
- power over production, people on whom the organisation depends to produce the service but whom it cannot control without ultimately an element of consent
- power over the environment in which the organisation operates, whether through direct regulation, general legislation or influence on the market place.

Figure 4.2 suggests a stakeholder map appropriate to public sector organisations. There could be debate about whether every stakeholder is placed in the correct segment. However, the map is offered not as a definitive statement but as a framework, or starting point, to help people to think about who their stakeholders might be. It does not matter where they fall on this diagram, the important thing is that the important stakeholders are all identified.

❑ The analysis

The basic steps of a stakeholder analysis, set out in Figure 4.3, are quite straightforward. The whole exercise can be completed, and often is, in an hour or so.

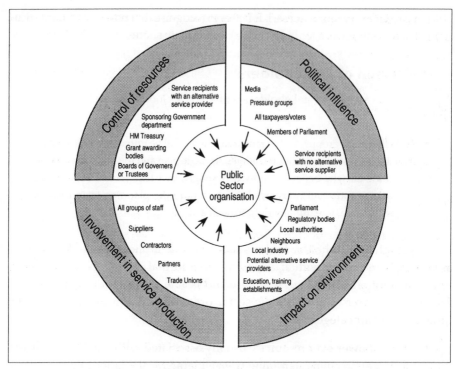

Figure 4.2. A public sector stakeholder map.

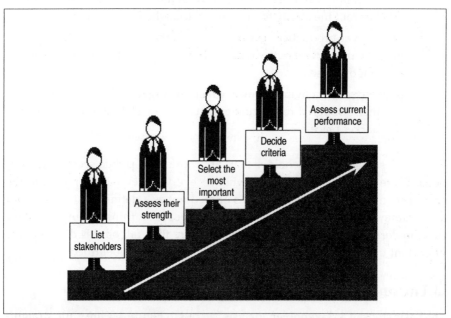

Figure 4.3. Steps in a stakeholder analysis.

Such a perfunctory approach, undertaken by a management team alone during a 24 or 36 hour retreat, could be a serious mistake. The risk, which recurs at many stages in the strategic management process, is that managers concentrate on consensus, on reaching agreement among themselves, and can easily reinterpret the world as they would like it to be rather than recognising it as it is. The approach described here is designed to reduce that risk.

List stakeholders

As explained in the previous chapter, a stakeholder analysis tends to be associated with the strategic planning rather than with the business planning cycle within the strategic management process. It is therefore undertaken only every few years. When it is agreed that a new strategic plan should be prepared, a vital first step is for the management team to agree what form the planning process should take, in effect to agree the 'project plan.' It is at this stage that they should also agree the list of stakeholders. This will then allow the planning staff to go and collect information about those stakeholders, to inform the stakeholder analysis.

Assess their strength and select the most important

At the end of the day, continuing with the pragmatic approach, it will be necessary to decide which of these stakeholders are likely to matter most, particularly if different stakeholders are likely to judge the organisation's performance according to different criteria. It is probably helpful, when listing the stakeholders, to take a view of their strength at the same time. This will enable those who then need to collect information on the stakeholders to concentrate their efforts on those likely to be of greatest importance.

Decide the criteria and assess current performance

What do the stakeholders expect from us? What criteria do they use when judging our performance? It is at this stage that information collected from the stakeholders needs to be available. Some of this may be collected regularly as a matter of routine, for example, from user surveys or regular feedback meetings with a sponsoring Government department or with the trade union side. In other cases special effort may be required to collect the information and/or to collate it in a form where it can be looked at objectively. The risk in a stakeholder analysis is that the management team simply record their present perceptions whereas any planning cycle must be used as an opportunity to stand back and change perceptions if necessary. Therefore, if we wish to record the criteria used by stakeholders to judge our performance and to record their views of our performance, we need to ask them. Nor should we forget that the operational staff may be nearer to many stakeholders than are the management team, so they too could contribute to the stakeholder analysis.

A further point at this stage is that, for a strategic plan, the concern is with the future rather than the present. We should be concerned not only with the criteria currently used by stakeholders but also with the criteria likely to be used in future. Sounding out the stakeholders about how their requirements are likely to change can be particularly helpful.

Recording the results

Figure 4.4 offers a form which could be useful for recording the outcome of a stakeholder analysis. Before using such a form any organisation should first check that it meets their particular requirements. There are one or two points which might be worth consideration.

Firstly, the form suggests a single score of importance for each stakeholder. It would be possible instead to score the importance of each of the individual criteria.

Secondly, the form records *current* performance against the criteria likely to be used in *future*. Current performance has the advantage of being factual, more objective. However, it may be worth asking how our performance would appear in future if we continued with current policies and strategies.

Thirdly, many criteria will be common to more than one stakeholder. The number of times a particular criterion recurs will itself contain a message about core objectives.

Finally, in the ratings of current performance, there is a category of 'don't know'. It seems doubtful whether such a marking would be acceptable for a stakeholder of any importance. The message of a 'don't know' would be 'go and find out'.

Draft aims and core objectives

The purpose of both the mandates analysis and the stakeholder analysis is to formulate a first draft of the role and purpose of the organisation. What are people expecting from us? What have we been set up to do? How would we define success? In our model of the strategic management process we have suggested that the answers to these questions are expressed in the form of a draft aim and some draft core objectives, core objectives being about underlying purpose, in contrast to change objectives, which reflect things which need to be achieved in order better to meet that underlying purpose.

Stakeholder Analysis

Name of stakeholder

Present importance	Likely future importance	Criteria currently used to judge performance	Current performance	Criteria likely to be used in future to judge performance	Current performance

KEY

Importance
1 – extremely important
2 – important
3 – of some importance
4 – of minor importance

Current Performance
VG – very good
G – good
OK – satisfactory
P – poor
VP – very poor
DK – don't know

Figure 4.4. Recording the outcome of a stakeholder analysis.

The subject of what makes a good aim and a good objective is covered in detail in Chapter 9. At this stage, however, quality of drafting is not important, the prime requirement is clarity and a measure of agreement on underlying purpose and the direction which the organisation needs to take. This can be expressed in a number of ways:

- a vision statement
- a mission statement
- a list of duties or responsibilities
- a single statement of aim
- a set of strategic objectives.

A danger with any of these is that time and effort could be diverted into issues of drafting. If such effort is genuinely helping to obtain clarity, it is worthwhile. There is a risk, though, that attempts to reach agreement on a draft are achieving the exact opposite of clarity, producing a form of words which everyone can accept, either because they can be interpreted in different ways or because they do not clearly commit anyone to anything. Effort devoted to this type of drafting in a strategic planning exercise almost certainly reveals a strategic problem in itself, a lack of agreement and team working among senior managers.

There is another reason why too much effort should not be devoted to drafting at this stage. A first draft is necessary to inform the next stages in the strategic management process, but those later stages may suggest that the initial drafts have to be amended. In practice, the writer has often found it helpful at this stage to concentrate on a simple statement of duties, the 'musts' from the mandates analysis, plus a series of short bullet points. As an illustration the bullet points for a Magistrates' Court may look something like the following:

- local, lay system of justice
- fair to all
- courteous, helpful
- bring cases to court promptly
- collect fines and fees promptly
- continuing improvement in costs per case
- facilities to meet needs of court users
- public confidence.

Others may like to add something more visionary, for example:

- a reputation as one of the top ten courts in the country.

Others may like to add verbs or adverbs which say more about a desired direction of change, such as:

- better facilities for court users
- greater public confidence
- reduce delays in bringing cases to court
- avoid any increase in backlog of fines and fees.

The choice must depend on the particular circumstances of the organisation and on its culture. Putting in writing a wish to be the best in the world is not in itself likely to inspire people, indeed it may be counterproductive if they feel it to be hopelessly ambitious or to distract attention from doing their own job. A visionary statement is only likely to be effective as a small part of a wider programme to create a visionary culture.

References

Argenti, J. (1993) *Your Organisation: What is it for?* Maidenhead, McGraw-Hill

Bryson, J. (1988) *Strategic Planning for Public and Nonprofit Organisations* London, Jossey-Bass

Goodstein, L. D. Nolan, T .M. and Pfeiffer, J. W. (1992) *Applied Strategic Planning: A Comprehensive Guide* San Diego, Pfeiffer and Company

Chapter 5

Analysing the external environment

The various planning techniques and approaches used within strategic management which are described in this book have been divided between four sections:

- external analysis
- internal analysis
- identifying issues
- action planning.

In practice, most of these techniques and approaches can be used in different ways and at different stages, the divisions used here just represent the author's view of where each technique has particular value. As each is discussed, reference will be made to its wider uses. There is also a short section at the end of each chapter which points to the other techniques which could be useful in the context of that chapter.

The analysis of the external environment, as indicated in Figure 3.2, is focused on answering the questions:

- how is the world likely to change
- what implications does this have for us
- in particular, given what we wish to be, how will these changes work for us or against us?

With this in mind, we will look in particular at:

- PEST
- forecasting models (time series and econometric models)
- market research
- focus groups
- Delphi
- scenarios.

PEST

PEST is an example of those planning 'techniques' which involve little more than identifying a list of topics which ought to be addressed. The 7– S framework and SWOT analysis, described in later chapters, are further examples. The purpose of following an approach such as PEST is to ensure that topics which have been found by others to be important are not left out of our consideration.

PEST is a mnemonic, the letters standing for:

P olitical

E conomic

S ocial

T echnological

The letters are sometimes rearranged to form the mnemonic STEP instead, which may have a less negative feel to it than PEST. We should be looking for trends in our favour, as well as trends working against us!

❑ The basic approach

The basic idea of PEST analysis is to:

- take each of the four elements in turn
- identify possible trends which could affect our organisation
- seek to establish the most likely trend or the range of most likely trends
- think through what their impact on our organisation would be if we were to continue into the future with our present strategies.

Figure 5.1 illustrates some of the subject areas which might need to be thought about in relation to the four key elements of a PEST analysis. As with most checklists, there is potential overlap between items and scope for debate on the heading under which any individual item is best located. For example, is control on public expenditure a political or an economic issue? The important thing is that an item should be covered in the debate, not where it falls in the listing! The list in Figure 5.1 may be a useful starting point, but the first step in a PEST analysis should be to review it and produce a list which seems appropriate to our own organisation. It may be that a set of main headings more appropriate than PEST can be found. Chapter 14 gives an example of an analysis based on the idea of

PEST but using some headings felt to be more germane to the Civil Service College; training methods were substituted for the technological and competition for social.

There may appear to be one obvious omission from the box headed 'political' in Figure 5.1, namely 'change of Government', or a change of political control. This can naturally be of enormous significance for some public sector organisations. Should public sector organisations reflect in current decisions the possibility of

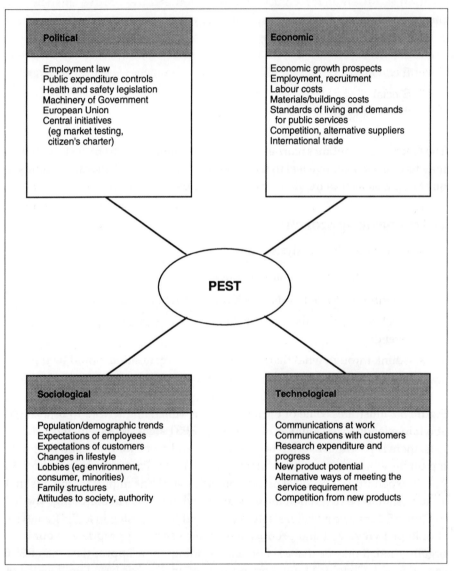

Figure 5.1. PEST analysis.

a Government of a different political party? Clearly, a private sector company might well wish to take decisions which may not be ideal for its shareholder if a present Government were to remain in power but which make it better equipped for success if that Government were voted out of office. A non-departmental public body could well wish to follow a similar course; its existence and responsibilities may be enshrined in legislation, voted by Parliament, and therefore with a degree of independence of the party in power. However, the position is different for civil servants, whether in executive agencies or Government departments, because they are employed by the Crown, in effect the Government, and their responsibility is therefore to the current ministers. Anything which could be interpreted as active preparation for a different Government might be considered unacceptable. Managers need to be aware of this issue, but debate on the matter is best left to public administration specialists and constitutional lawyers.

❏ The participants

Who should be involved in PEST analysis? Certainly the management team should be actively involved, but a wider involvement is strongly advised. There remains the danger that the management team's perspective could be narrow or that they have a tendency to interpret the world

- as they would like it to be, or
- as they have always assumed it to be.

Involving some groups of junior staff may well be beneficial, because they could have a different perspective arising from the different nature of their contact with the recipient of the service. Members of any non-executive board ought to be able to play a particularly valuable role in a PEST analysis. They are likely to have been selected on the grounds of their ability to bring a wider perspective to the management of the organisation, and they should be able to warn the executive management, from a more detached viewpoint, of the possible implications of wider political, economic, social and technical trends.

The final point to make about PEST analysis is that it does not have to stand alone. It will be more powerful when combined with other techniques described later:

- Delphi techniques may be useful in the forward-looking aspect of PEST
- use of focus groups could involve a wider range of particularly knowledgeable people in the analysis
- introducing some time series and econometric and market research work may help to make the analysis more soundly informed.

Forecasting models

This is one of the few points in the strategic management process where management may find that they have to call in and rely on experts. In applying most of the techniques managers may benefit from the use of a facilitator who has broader experience of using them, but the techniques do not themselves require specialist knowledge. The effective use of forecasting models, does, however, require some understanding of mathematics and statistics. In what follows we attempt no more than to explain in very broad terms what these techniques can and cannot do. This carries a health warning; if you feel that you could benefit from using these techniques, consult your nearest expert practitioner.

❏ Time series analysis

A starting point is to think in terms of looking at how the demand for the organisation's services has moved in the past. As an example, take the hypothetical series illustrated in Figure 5.2a. If the current year is signified by year 0, it can be seen that the number of cases coming forward has risen from 235 nine years ago to 443 in the current year. Plotting the data seems to suggest that the number of cases has risen more or less in a straight line. It does not need much statistical knowledge to take a ruler and draw a straight line, as in Figure 5.2b, which fits as closely as possible to the data points, nor does it require advanced mathematics to work out that growth has averaged something like 25 additional cases each year.

The statistician will, in fact, be able to do something more rigorous than that. It is possible to estimate by statistical methods (regression analysis), a mathematical equation of the straight line which fits the points most closely, and it is also possible to obtain a measure of *how* closely the line fits the points. The statistician will then be able to give advice along the following lines:

> *if past trends continue into the future*, there is a 95% probability that, in five years'
> time, you will have to deal with something between 540 and 610 cases.

The words in italics are critically important. Whether we have used a ruler or a statistician, extending the relationship into the future, as illustrated by the dotted section of the line in Figure 5.2b, involves a sweeping assumption that nothing about the future will result in a different annual growth from that observed in the past. It should be emphasised that the statistician is not restricted to fitting straight lines, it is perfectly possible to fit exponential curves, or S-curves, or other types of curve, but none of this alters the fact that one is assuming that the growth pattern in the future will be the same as that identified from the past.

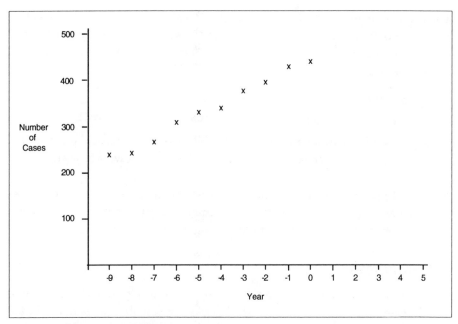

Figure 5.2a. Trend in number of cases through time.

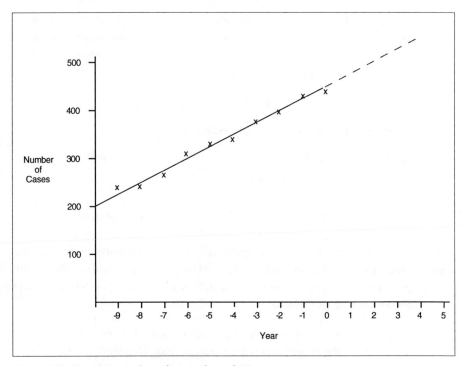

Figure 5.2b. Trend in number of cases through time.

The illustration given above is very simple and seriously undersells the potential power of time series analysis. Thorough statistical analysis of past data may be capable of detecting patterns which are highly likely to be repeated in the future, for example:

- monthly or quarterly seasonal patterns
- regular cycles, perhaps two or three year cycles
- dependence of the present on what happened at a particular point in the past, as when some of the cases are in fact renewals of past cases.

It is easy to see how this could be helpful to an activity such as issuing passports. Knowledge of seasonal patterns of demand can inform planning by showing how speed of service can be traded off against the use of seasonal labour.

❏ Econometric analysis

Having moved from the very simple extrapolation of Figure 5.2b to the more sophisticated time series analysis which looks for less obvious patterns in the data, the next step is to try to understand the reasons lying behind the year to year fluctuations in the number of cases coming forward in the past. What economic and/or social variables explain sudden increases or decreases in the number of cases? The statistician, again using regression analysis or related techniques, will be able to use past data to estimate an equation which relates the number of cases coming forward, Y, to any economic or social factors which managers would like to try. It might, for example, produce an equation such as:

$$\Delta Y = 20 - 5\Delta GDP + 10\Delta\left(\frac{R}{R^*}\right) + 2\Delta S$$

where Δ signifies change over previous year

GDP = gross domestic profit
R = actual winter rainfall
R* = normal winter rainfall
S = number of students leaving school with no qualifications.

This analysis of past data certainly contributes to an understanding of what *has* affected the number of cases and can help managers to understand the uncertainty about future figures. How useful is it, though, for forecasting the future? Three factors limit its usefulness.

(i) As the equation will never fit the data perfectly it leaves part of the variation in the number of cases unexplained. Therefore the forecast must be in the form of a range of figures, such as, 'we can be 95% certain that the figure will be somewhere between 420 and 510.'

(ii) To use the equation to produce a forecast for the future, it is necessary first to forecast gross domestic product, rainfall and the number of students leaving school with no qualifications. How reliable will those forecasts be?

(iii) It is implicitly assumed that the relationship with gross domestic product, rainfall and student qualifications which has been observed in the past will hold for the future as well.

The first of the problems is not too serious, as long as the range quoted is not so wide that it fails to help to narrow down the options for the future. The second problem is more serious, because it may mean that the range of uncertainty associated with the forecast may not be known at all. The third can be extremely serious. It means that ultimately, despite any amount of sophisticated quantitative work, it is necessary to rely on a large element of judgement as to:

- whether past relationships will hold in the future
- the implications for trends in the number of cases if they do not.

It is now almost customary to illustrate these problems with reference to forecasts of oil demand, as generally indicated by Figure 5.3. During the 1950s the rate of growth kept rising, and forecasts tended to extrapolate current growth and were always conservative. The forecasts happily extrapolated growth rates into the 1970s and failed to anticipate the turning point in the early 1970s. Despite that experience, the same problems emerged again in the late 1970s and early 1980s.

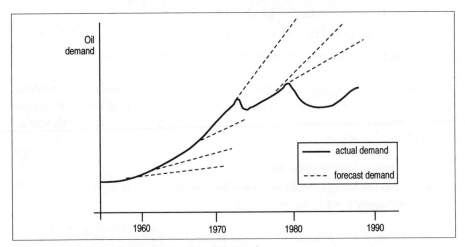

Figure 5.3. Actual and forecast world oil demand.

So should we just abandon statistical methods? Certainly not. Rigorous analysis of past data will help to improve understanding of the key factors in the environment. What is more, without this rigour we may well end up interpreting past experience in a way which suits our preconceptions, rather than understanding it as it really is. Managers should do all they can to ensure that past data are carefully analysed and conclusions objectively presented. Having done that, however, a major element of subjective judgement will still be necessary to decide on the most likely trends for the future. Market research, focus groups and the use of Delphi techniques can all make a contribution towards improving that judgement.

Market research

Market research can be used for both external and internal analysis. In the former case our attention will be concentrated on:

- national trends in the demand or need for the services which we provide
- trends in factors known from any statistical work to be important determinants of the demand for the service
- views about which aspects of the service are growing or declining in importance
- views on any alternatives to the service which might be available
- the actions of and others' attitudes towards any competitors.

When we turn to internal analysis, the emphasis switches to views about

- the service which our own particular organisation provides
- what people like or dislike about it
- how they perceive it relative to any alternatives
- whether they have heard of us and understand what we do.

In the case of a public sector organisation which has a monopoly of a particular service, with no alternatives and no competitors, the external and internal elements of the market research may be virtually indistinguishable. In this section we shall look briefly at:

- sources of market research
- some key principles of research design and analysis which senior managers need to keep in mind.

The emphasis, at this point, is on market research as part of the external analysis stage of the planning cycle.

❏ Sources of market research

The words 'market research' may immediately bring to mind the idea of commissioning some special work from one of the well-known companies associated with public opinion polls. That is probably the most expensive option, and other possibilities might be considered first. The range of options would include:

- regularly published statistics
- scanning by a library or information service
- buying in to a regular on-going survey
- specific surveys by an in-house team
- a specific study by a market research firm

As we go down the list, the items tend to become less specific but also less costly.

Published statistics

A wide range of statistics is published regularly by Government and by other bodies such as trade associations and sometimes commercial companies. Some of the commercial or quasi-commercial organisations even produce forecasts of key variables for the future. In many cases the need to view and review these statistics on a regular basis is obvious and taken for granted. It would be somewhat surprising if the Employment Service were to fail to take a close interest in the unemployment statistics and in the forecasts of the economy made by the various economic forecasting groups (including the Treasury, of course!) However, there may be other cases where the potential of the available statistics has not been fully exploited. It has to be accepted, though, that the information collected actually may not always fit too well with what an individual organisation needs.

Scanning by a library or information service

In the writer's experience, the information service capability of library staff is a much underused resource, in central Government at least. Information relevant to an organisation might emerge not from a regular source, such as a statistical publication, but from irregular sources, such as newspaper reports, occasional articles in journals, new pamphlets or books. Many people may be familiar with a newspaper abstracting service which helps to keep them up to date with press comment on their areas of responsibility, but this service can easily be extended to cover both wider subjects relevant to an organisation's external environment and a wider range of sources.

Buying into a regular survey

Market research surveys are expensive, particularly if they require face-to-face interviews. The fixed cost per interview can make surveys prohibitively expensive if you only have a few questions to ask. There are, however, many market research companies who undertake large scale surveys on a regular basis, and it is possible to purchase 'space' in such a survey. Readers may be acquainted with some public sector surveys, which have worked in this way, for example the General Household Survey. Individual Government departments were invited to suggest, or 'bid for', questions to add to the basic core. The market research companies do undertake some surveys which concentrate on particular subject areas, for example, there is one which covers trends in, attitudes to and demands for management training, which the Civil Service College has found useful.

Buying in to a regular survey can be a very cost-effective way of obtaining information on changes in demands, attitudes and perceptions on an ongoing basis. Remember that strategic management is an ongoing activity, not a once a year or once every three years activity.

Specific surveys

Specific surveys may be undertaken either by an in-house team or by a market research firm. Using an in-house team would tend to be a stronger possibility where:

- the team has a fund of expertise in questionnaire and survey design
- there is a readily identifiable group of people to survey
- the questions are straightforward and suited for a postal survey.

If it is important to obtain a random sample from the population as a whole, or if professional interviewers are required, it will almost certainly be advisable to call on the professional skills of a specialist research organisation. Central Government does, of course, already have a great deal of survey expertise, and the Office of Population Censuses and Surveys is able to offer both advice on and assistance with surveys.

❏ Some key principles of research design and analysis

In the opening chapters a great deal of stress was laid on the principle that strategic management is a continuous process. Data gathering is not therefore something which has to be done only when a new plan has to be prepared. Strategic management requires managers throughout an organisation to be continuously aware of trends which should influence their decisions. Therefore:

- market research should be an ongoing activity
- its results should be regularly available to all managers

- but it is helpful if, at the analysis stage of the strategic management process, the experience of recent research is consolidated by the planning team into a single document for the information of those involved in the analysis.

These principles apply to regular surveys, published statistics, and to abstracting services. When it comes to preparing a new plan, people will have picked up some general impressions from the abstracts, but they could be unduly influenced by one or two specific reports. Memories could also be vague if the flow of information is both large and regular. A careful analysis which concentrates on main trends but includes reminders to key items can be extremely useful in focusing the debate at management team level.

When it comes to analysing data from surveys, life is very much easier if the questions were structured in such a way that the results can be expressed in a quantitative form. This normally requires multiple choice questions, meaning that those designing the questionnaire pre-specify the possible answers. The danger with this, from the strategic planning point of view, is that it may prevent respondents from saying what they would really like to say. This is a very subtle way in which managers can interpret the world as they would like it to be rather than as it really is! A way to reduce this risk, while obtaining results in a structured form, is to undertake some unstructured interviews first, to establish the range of answers which people want to offer, and then use those answers to form the multiple choice options.

Questionnaire design is not as simple as might be thought. Ultimately it is a matter of common sense, but people do in practice find it very difficult to put themselves in the position of others and recognise how others could interpret a question. If an organisation wishes to design its own questionnaire it is always advisable to ask someone experienced in designing and using questionnaires at the very least to cast an eye over a draft. Government departments which regularly conduct large-scale surveys will have their own in-house expertise, others can always call upon the Office of Population Censuses and Surveys for advice. Then, never skimp on the pilot survey, although everyone is always tempted to do so. The pilot survey will quickly show where questions are confusing people, particularly if you give them a good opportunity to report back on their difficulties in completing the questionnaire.

The choice and size of sample is not an easy matter either. Whole books have been written on the subject, so suffice it to say here that expert advice should be sought. It is regrettably too easy to conduct an expensive survey, only to find that the size of sample chosen is not capable of giving you the level of accuracy which you need in the results.

Focus groups

It is not difficult to convince managers that they need to take some account of the external environment in drawing up their plans for the future. There will be differences of view about the effort appropriate to the external analysis, ranging from those who feel that they can significantly mould their environment to those who regard themselves as slaves to their environment. Either way, though, it is suggested that any external analysis undertaken needs to have:

- breadth
- objectivity.

Breadth requires the collection of all of the data which are relevant. Objectivity requires careful analysis of the data, letting the data speak rather than using them to support an already written story. Focus groups contribute to breadth, by enlarging the range of people, opinions and expertise which are called upon. We shall look briefly at the appropriate membership of focus groups and at some principles for making effective use of those groups.

❏ Membership

The very word 'focus' suggests that the members should have a common interest. This interest may be:

- a specific professional expertise
- a particular shared experience
- a common interest in a particular subject
- a common interest in the organisation.

An example of the first could be academic scientists. If a research council wished to think about trends in academic research, it may well choose to call together a group of respected academic scientists for advice. Perhaps the Chancellor of the Exchequer's group of 'wise men' who advise on economic forecasts fit into this category. The second group, those with shared experience, might consist, for example, of people who have all faced opposition from a particular type of lobby or who have all considered the prospect of raising private funding. The third group could be exemplified by representatives of environmental pressure groups, or people who work for voluntary organisations devoted to the care of children. The fourth type of focus group may be composed of representatives of the organisation's workforce, of its customers, or of its principal stakeholders.

The management team and the planners will need to think through what would be the most useful type of group in the light of the organisation's own specific circumstances. In the extreme it could even be right to take a random sample of the general public, even if it might be difficult to classify the gathering as a 'focus group'. However, such a group might be more appropriate for the internal analysis, where the organisation might be interested in how it is perceived by the taxpayer generally. In the external analysis, we should be looking for a group of people who, by reason of expertise or interest, can add to the knowledge of the management team about the external environment.

❏ Effective use of the group

The key choice faced is the extent to which any discussion should be structured, rather than left to range freely. Should there be:

- a clear agenda
- a few specified subject areas
- an entirely free ranging debate?

It is unlikely that the last of these would be very effective. The organisation will have particular areas of interest which it would wish to see addressed in preference to the price of coffee. In contrast, a detailed agenda and tight management should ensure useful information on the subjects which the organisers have chosen. The danger is that it gives the participants no opportunity to say:

> this is all very well but have you thought about the potential impact of .....?

Needless to say, the middle ground has much to commend it. This would probably take the form of a structured agenda, with a reasonable amount of time left for the participants to respond to the invitation:

> is there anything else which you would like to add, anything which you feel that we should be taking into account?

Those organising the meeting will also wish to ensure that they get as much value as possible from every participant. There is a danger in any group meeting that some personalities will dominate the discussion, with others, who may have some excellent ideas, feeling too intimidated to offer them. This issue is discussed under the headings of SWOT analysis in Chapter 7 and brainstorming in Chapter 8. The ideas suggested there apply equally well to focus groups. The use of Delphi techniques, discussed below, might also be helpful.

Focus groups have been included as an approach to external analysis, but group discussions of this type can be used at a number of points in the strategic planning process. Such groups can be used whenever there is a desire to call on a range of expertise or interest, or simply where there is a wish to involve people, reflect their views and gain their commitment to the final outcome. Particular points at which such groups might be used are:

- developing scenarios
- discussion of the 7–S framework
- building up life cycle or portfolio analyses
- constructing value chains
- SWOT analysis.

Delphi

The Delphi technique was developed at the RAND Corporation of Santa Monica in the 1950s. The emphasis in the original project was on defence applications and on establishing a degree of consensus amongst experts on answers to questions where the answers inevitably required a heavy measure of judgement. The technique has potentially wide applications but has been used particularly for technological forecasting. In the present context, the emphasis is on its potential for helping to clarify possible developments where there is little evidence from hard information or where there is serious concern that experience from the past may be of very limited value in forecasting the future.

The aim in using Delphi techniques is to reach a reasonable degree of consensus in a controlled way. In its purer forms, the process would probably follow something like the sequence set out in Figure 5.4. The key features are:

- anonymity, no attribution
- controlled feedback
- opportunities for revision of opinions.

It should be emphasised that the emphasis is on reaching a degree of consensus. Whether this consensus represents a good forecast of the future trends will depend heavily on the quality of perceptions of those on the panel and on whether their thinking is allowed to embrace all of the possibilities. The technique is designed to help in this regard by at least ensuring, through the anonymity, that one or two individuals with strong views and/or personalities do not dominate the conclusions.

❑ The participants

If an organisation does feel that a process broadly along the lines set out in Figure 5.4 could be helpful, a prime question is:

how should the panel be constituted?

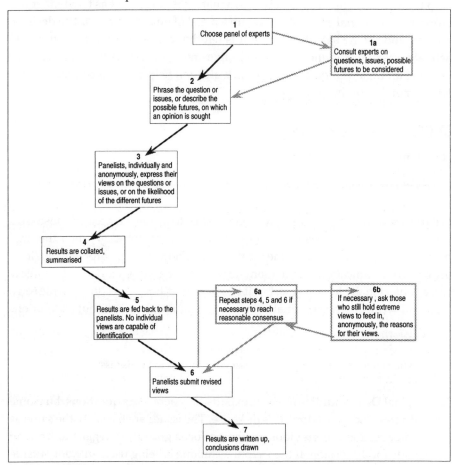

Figure 5.4. Delphi technique.

Originally the Delphi technique assumed the use of experts, but it can also be used to try to achieve consensus among management teams or groups of an organisation's own staff. There are some dangers in using only the management team:

- the range of thinking may be limited, by small numbers, by past peer pressure, or by the limited range of experience of the broader external environment
- anonymity may be difficult to preserve.

Although answers and views may be unattributed, it may be easy to say:

> I know who must have said that!

Using a broader cross-section of the organisation's own staff should normally help to ease these difficulties. It is then a matter of judgement as to whether it is worth the additional effort of setting up a panel of outside experts. The decision will depend on the extent to which it is felt that a cross-section of staff would actually offer a broad enough and objective enough perspective. An advantage of using an organisation's own staff is that it can help to build commitment to and ownership of the outcome.

❏ Effective use of the group

A first question to be addressed is:

> should we eventually allow some direct social contact between the participants?

If there are differences of view and one wishes to achieve a greater consensus, the reasons for the views need to be shared. That is not easy when the only medium of communication is the written word. However, the problem of allowing oral communication is that anonymity is lost. It may be worthwhile to allow some contact in the later stages, but it is probably still wise to allow people to go back and write down their final answers and submit them without attribution.

A second question is:

> who should frame the questions, issues or futures to be discussed?

The original Delphi studies used the experts to generate the questions, but some other studies since have done this in-house. The issues are basically the same as those addressed in the previous section on focus groups, in regard to framing the agenda for discussion. If the Delphi technique is being used without outside panellists, it may well be worthwhile to ensure that an outside facilitator has at least some input into framing the questions.

❏ Other uses of Delphi

Given that it is designed to move a group of people towards consensus, the Delphi technique may be valuable at a number of other points in the strategic management process. At any point where there is a group discussion, it can be used if it is wished to move towards consensus rather than just to sound out opinion. Particular points where the technique is most likely to be useful include:

- PEST analysis
- SWOT analysis
- creating options
- appraising options
- creating scenarios.

Scenarios

A scenario has been defined by Leemhuis (1990) as:

> a coherent story about the business environment with the world of today as the
> starting point .... Ideally a scenario should be a description of a possible future in
> which social, political, economic and technological developments evolve in an
> internally consistent order.

The use of scenarios has been associated with the problems of planning in an uncertain environment, when there is a need to recognise the possibility that the world of tomorrow could be radically different from the world of today. Thinking about the future, there may be many different sources of uncertainty, fuel prices, economic growth, social attitudes, levels of public expenditure, and so on. However, these sources of uncertainty are not independent of each other. If fuel prices rise rapidly they will have an impact on economic growth and this could in turn affect social attitudes. This is why there is an emphasis when building scenarios on the idea of internal consistency, building a picture which is coherent.

❏ The uses of scenarios

Scenarios can be used in three direct ways in the strategic management process:

- identifying issues facing the organisation as a result of possible developments in the external environment
- as an aid to appraising options, offering different pictures of the future against which alternative strategies can be appraised
- in building options for the future for appraisal.

An example of the third of these uses is given in Chapter 14. Different pictures of the future organisation are constructed, and the preferred one is chosen, thus determining the organisation's vision of itself, setting the goal towards which it is striving. The second use of scenarios involves asking how different options for the future compare in each scenario of the external environment in turn. One option may look good in a high growth scenario, another may look good in a low growth scenario; however, a third may be preferred, if the organisation tends to be risk averse, if it looks reasonable against either scenario. At this point in the book we are principally concerned with the use of scenarios in raising issues associated with developments in the outside world. However, once scenarios have been constructed for this purpose, they can be used subsequently for the second.

It is often said that one of the main benefits of scenario building is that it helps to change managers' ways of thinking. Scenarios are best built by managers, probably with the help of skilled facilitation. In this way they are forced to think about how the world could change, and forced to think hard, not simply extrapolate. They come to realise that one adverse trend can easily lead to another, and that both together could well necessitate drastic changes in the demand for present services. This knowledge will then alter their day-to-day management decisions, and should be making them better managers, as well as helping them to identify issues which need to be addressed in the planning process.

❑ Some principles of scenario building

Building scenarios is not about trying to build the most likely picture of the future, a single future. The idea is to build some different pictures of the future, but each one internally consistent.

One way of starting is to identify a few key themes, which reflect the major uncertainties about the future. Examples might be:

- the rate of economic growth
- the level of public support for a particular pressure group
- political decisions about public expenditure priorities
- the level of competition, the growth of activities which may reduce the need for the service which we provide.

Then scenarios could be constructed around these themes. If the themes were independent of each other (eg the rate of economic growth had no effect on pressure groups, expenditure priorities and competition) this would leave a large number of potential scenarios. In fact, if each theme had two possibilities, one high, one low, there would be 16 combinations. Constructing 16 complete scenarios, describing what each would mean, could take a little time and would then produce so much information as to confuse rather than illuminate. The normal advice is to limit the scenarios to a small number, at least two and probably not more than four. In practice this means that the underlying themes tend to end up as optimism and pessimism. Many writers suggest three scenarios, optimistic, pessimistic, and one in-between. The problem with this is that the middle one automatically tends to be interpreted as the most likely and is accorded the greatest attention in any subsequent analysis. The present writer therefore prefers to use four scenarios if possible.

Although in building scenarios use can be made of quantitative information, the scenario pictures, or descriptions, should be primarily qualitative. Expressing them in quantitative form could give the impression of accuracy and lead those building and using them to fail to recognise the true level of uncertainty and its implications. For similar reasons, no attempt should be made to attach a level of probability to each scenario.

It has already been suggested that managers should be involved in building scenarios. However, the more complex the business, the more likely it is that the scenarios will need to be constructed initially by multi-disciplinary teams, bringing together experience of different parts of the organisation. Senior managers, though, need to be brought into the discussion and fully understand the scenarios before they are used.

Constructing scenarios involves trying to build consensus. Therefore Delphi techniques are sometimes used in the process.

Other techniques for external analysis

The theory of competitive advantage has been included in Chapter 7, because it tends to point directly to strategic issues and to conclusions about the forms which strategies should take. However, its starting point is an analysis of the industry structure, which is approached through the concept of the 'five forces'. That concept can be used in itself to structure thinking about the external environment, about the 'industry' in which we are operating. In Chapter 7 the five forces are considered in a public sector context.

Benchmarking, explained in the next chapter, concentrates primarily on an organisation's own performance, and has therefore been classified primarily as a technique for internal analysis. However, one aspect of benchmarking is performance relative to competitors, and this can generate external information, on developments in any markets in which we are competing with others.

References and further reading

Dalkey, N. C. (1969) *The Delphi Method: An Experimental Study of Group Opinion* Santa Monica, Cal. RAND Corporation

Parenté, F. J. and Anderson-Parenté, J. K. (1987) *Delphi Inquiry Systems* in ed Wright, G. and Ayton, P. *Judgmental Forecasting* Chichester, John Wiley & Sons

Leemhuis, J. P. (1990) *Using scenarios to develop strategies at Shell* in Taylor, B. and Harrison, J. *The Manager's Casebook of Business Strategy* Oxford, Butterworth-Heinemann

Chapter 6

Internal analysis

We now turn to techniques which help, as suggested in Figure 3.2, to answer the questions:

> what are the things about ourselves which are likely to help us or hinder us in our attempts to be what we want to be?

The techniques which will be described all concentrate primarily on considering whether the organisation is:

- doing the right things
- doing them well

and, if it is not,

- what is it about the organisation which is holding it back?

The specific techniques discussed are:

- benchmarking
- the Boston portfolio matrix
- product life cycles
- value chain analysis
- the 7-S framework.

Benchmarking

You want your company to be a world beater? Of course you do. But where do you start? Or, to put it another way, how do you know whether your company now is good, bad, indifferent or at the top of the league in the things that matter in your sector of industry?

The answer to both questions lies in Best Practice Benchmarking or BPB. BPB is a technique used by successful companies around the world – in all sectors of business, both manufacturing and service – to help them become good or better than the best in the world in the most important aspects of their operations. Many of these companies are multi-national giants, such as Ford, ICI, Nissan or Xerox. Others are small businesses employing a handful of people. They all have one thing in common: a recognition that profitability and growth come from a clear understanding of how the business is doing, not just against its own performance last year, but against the best they can measure.

That quotation from a booklet produced by the Department of Trade and Industry (1992) effectively summarises the idea of benchmarking. Basically it is a systematic attempt to compare our own organisation's performance with other organisations, but with an emphasis on comparison with the best, in order to identify where we can and should improve our own performance. It involves looking not so much at overall performance as at performance in particular key areas. This is how it helps us to identify issues to be addressed, areas to be tackled, in our own planning processes.

❏ Types of benchmarking

Types of benchmarking can be considered along two dimensions, as illustrated in Figure 6.1. The horizontal axis involves consideration of who our benchmarking partners should be, the vertical axis considers the aspects of performance which should be benchmarked. Each axis will be looked at in turn.

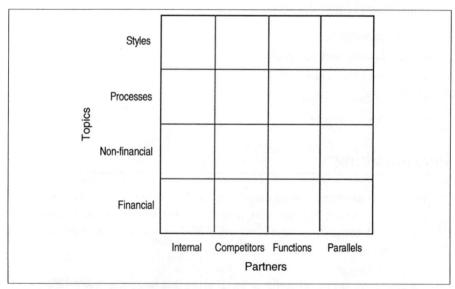

Figure 6.1. The benchmarking grid.

Benchmarking partners

In many ways, internal benchmarking is the most straightforward. If the same types of activities are being undertaken by different groups within the organisation, or by different individuals within the organisation, then performance of the groups or individuals can be compared. This can be seen as threatening by the groups and individuals concerned, but the purpose should be a constructive one, learning from the experience of others. Management style is very important here to engender a healthy competitive spirit and constructive debate rather than fierce competitiveness which can lead to secrecy and playing the numbers game. Internal benchmarking should be cheap, the data can be collected as part of the normal management information, and it should be possible to ensure consistency of definitions, for example, common practices in the allocation of costs. However, the basic requirement is that similar work is being done by different groups. There are many examples in the public sector where this condition is met, for example, payment of social security benefits, Customs and Excise, Inland Revenue, hospitals, schools, prisons and so on. A good example is the Management Information System of the Magistrates' Courts Service. Each court provides returns covering four key indicators of performance, backed by a substantial number of secondary indicators. Each court is able to compare its own performance with the best court in its category, the categories being defined to ensure that the comparisons are between courts which deal with similar types of workload. The Audit Commission's approach of defining a small number of performance indicators for each local authority service also enables a degree of benchmarking to take place.

Benchmarking against competitors has a fairly obvious potential pay-off, if one is seeking to establish a competitive advantage. It will not apply so much in the public sector; it is unusual for a public sector organisation to be in full competition with a range of other suppliers, but there can sometimes be strong competition over a range of services. The difficulty here is that there may be an understandable reluctance to share data, for fear of enabling a competitor to catch up! The potential for benchmarking against competitors tends to be limited to data which are published or which can be obtained indirectly or by inference. This means that benchmarking against organisations in other areas of business is of particular importance.

There are many activities which an organisation undertakes which mirror activities in organisations in quite different businesses. More obvious examples include:

- paying employees
- providing office accommodation

- cleaning buildings
- catering
- transport services
- the personnel function.

Much of the market testing activity in the public sector has reflected this idea of 'functional benchmarking,' though market testing goes further than benchmarking per se. When benchmarking against competitors or other organisations, care is necessary to ensure that any numerical data are constructed and defined in compatible ways.

Benchmarking with parallels tends to have less precision than benchmarking functions. A parallel organisation is one that has some generic feature in common with our own. For example, if we have to take a large number of bookings, it may be worth benchmarking with an airline or travel operator, if we have to impart a lot of information to a lot of people, it may be worth benchmarking against companies in the advertising business.

Benchmarking topics

Comparisons of financial performance and of key financial ratios have been common for many years. In recent years, in the private sector there has been an increasing emphasis on non-financial aspects of performance which are considered to be key pointers towards financial success, for example, delivery times, repeat business, market share, customer perceptions and so on. These are the 'hard' or 'relatively hard' aspects of performance. However, there is also a great deal to be learned by benchmarking 'softer' topics, such as the approach to managing a particular process. Benchmarking should be a learning process; establishing that another organisation has managed to reduce its stockholding to half of our own figure identifies an issue, tells us we could do better. What we really need to know, however, is how to do it. Benchmarking in this sense goes beyond collecting numbers and involves sharing information about processes.

The 'softest' end of the topics axis in Figure 6.1 is 'styles'. Looking at parallels, we might identify a particular company as excellent in satisfying and retaining the loyalty of its customers. How does it do it? It may be partly about processes (e.g. newsletters, special offers to existing customers) but it may also be partly about attitude, styles and cultures within the organisation. Benchmarking on 'styles' is again not about collection of numbers but about discussion, visits and direct observation.

❏ Applying benchmarking

It should be clear from the description of the types of benchmarking that it is not a technique to be used on a one-off basis whenever a new plan has to be prepared. Benchmarking needs to be a continuous process if it is to be used to maximum advantage. Taking stock of the latest data, however, and more formally reviewing recent trends is an important step in the planning process. The lack of benchmarking information could, of course, be noted as a key issue, a major weakness, in its own right.

The key steps in setting up a benchmarking process are suggested by the Department of Trade and Industry (1992) to be the following:

1. What are we going to benchmark?
2. Who are we going to benchmark against?
3. How will we get the information?
4. How will we analyse the information?
5. How will we use the information?

In deciding what to benchmark and who to benchmark against, the grid in Figure 6.1 might be helpful. Plot each item of benchmarking information in its appropriate box on the grid, and then look to see if the distribution makes sense. Is there too much financial information and not enough on styles? Is there too much functional comparison and not enough on competitors? These questions can only be answered by taking account of the circumstances of the particular organisation. There is no point in bemoaning the lack of information on competitors if there are none or the lack of internal comparisons if there are no cases of different groups doing the same type of work!

To private sector companies in a competitive market, comparisons of performance are an imperative for survival. Benchmarking perhaps adds a dimension to that by encouraging comparison with the best. In the public sector it has been possible to manage without such comparisons, but comparisons are the only way to provide evidence of value of money. The pressure for value for money from public expenditure is now making such comparisons an imperative in the public sector as well, that imperative driven home by the reality of market testing and the recognition of the potential for contracting out the actual delivery of public services. A similar argument about demonstration of value for money is made by Karlöf and Östblom (1993) in a private sector context:

> Large areas of our organised world exist in conditions of planned economy. Departments of companies make internal deliveries to users who in practice are not free to choose alterative suppliers. Although the result of a company at the aggregate level can be read from its accounts, there are many functional parts of it which are not subject to measurement of performance in terms of profit and loss.

Benchmarking offers a substitute for the spur to efficiency that is one of the functions of a free market economy. When the unseen hand of market forces is not there to compel efficiency (the function of value and productivity), benchmarking performs that function instead. The same thing applies to all tax-financed systems, which likewise lack the spur to efficiency of a free market-economy.

As mentioned at the end of Chapter 5, while benchmarking is felt to fit primarily within the category of internal analysis, information on the performance of competitors can also contribute to the external analysis.

The Boston matrix

The starting point for the Boston matrix is the concept of the experience curve. Stated simply (Henderson, 1984):

'cost of value added declines approximately 20 to 30 per cent, each time accumulated experienced is doubled.' This is an observable phenomenon. Whatever the reason, it happens.

The bases of this phenomenon are:

- *learning*, workers learn with experience how to perform tasks better
- *specialisation*, as scale increases tasks can be broken down, and each person can specialise on one part, do that part more frequently, and learn faster
- *investment*, capital is invested over time in order to reduce costs
- *scale*, equipment to produce twice the level of output does not normally cost twice as much.

The experience curve implies that a large market share tends to be associated with a low unit cost relative to competitors. In Henderson's words (1984):

A difference in market share of 2 to 1 should produce about 20 per cent or more differential in pre tax cost on value added.

This means that a high market share tends to be associated with an ability to generate larger positive cash flows.

Turning now to the demand for cash, it is the rate of growth of a product which tends to determine cash use. Growth demands cash for investment in additional capacity for production and distribution. Putting cash use (product growth) and cash generation (market share) together produces a 2 x 2 matrix, four quadrant diagram, Figure 6.2. The four quadrants are labelled:

cash cows   -   high market share, low growth, generating cash which helps to cover the organisation's overhead and contribute to investment, for the future, in stars

stars   -   high market share, high growth, they both use cash and generate cash and so may be broadly in balance in terms of net cash flow, but these are cash cows of the future as long as they do not lose market share

dogs   -   low market share, low growth, may be net cash users, will never contribute much but could make significant demands on management time

question marks   -   low market share, high growth, and therefore significant net users of cash; unless market share increases they will eventually become dogs and never repay the investment.

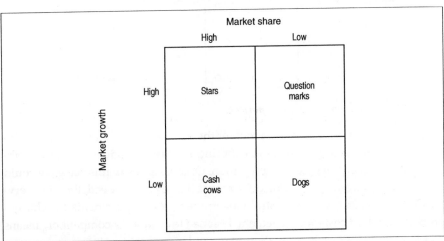

Figure 6.2. The Boston Consulting Group matrix.

So how would this matrix be used in the analysis stage of strategic management? Each product may be plotted on the diagram, each perhaps in the form of a circle where the diameter is proportional to turnover. This would give a picture such as that in Figure 6.3, representing a current portfolio. This particular portfolio would suggest the following:

- a strength is the number of cash cows.
- a weakness is the lack of stars, suggesting a risk of there being no cash cows in future

- the dog is a possible weakness, an issue is whether it should be retained
- a weakness is the number of question marks; this is an issue which will need resolving, should we try to change them into stars or should they be disposed of?

It may also be worthwhile to try to draw the diagram as it might appear in five years' time if current strategies were not changed.

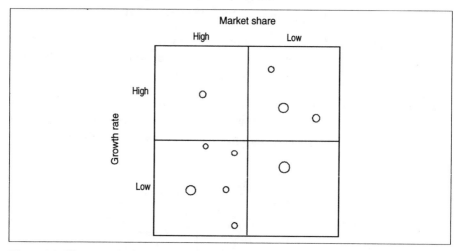

Figure 6.3. Illustration of a product portfolio.

The Boston matrix is essentially a tool for the private sector, but it could be helpful to any public sector organisation offering a range of products which are subject to at least some degree of competition. Organisations in this category could be Her Majesty's Stationery Office, Ordnance Survey and, indeed, the Civil Service College. In fact, within central Government, the requirements for charges properly to reflect costs, a requirement designed to ensure fair competition, means that the concept of cash generation may not be applicable. However, a matrix based on the two dimensions of growth rate and turnover may be useful in identifying whether the portfolio of products is a balanced one, both currently and for the future. If the majority of the turnover is in low growth products, there is certainly an issue to be addressed about future prospects.

Moving away from commercial or quasi-commercial organisations within the public sector, any organisation providing a range of services may find it useful to apply the matrix concept. A matrix with the dimensions growth of demand and current costs may produce a useful pictorial representation of potential pressure for the future. A matrix using the dimensions current costs and political sensitivity may help to highlight issues in the present allocation of resources between services.

Product life cycles

The product life cycle is an extremely simple concept, to many perhaps a simplistic one. The basic idea, which originated in the field of marketing, was that any product will tend to have a life cycle which follows a broadly similar pattern through four stages:

- launch
- growth
- maturity
- decline.

Graphically this might appear as in Figure 6.4.

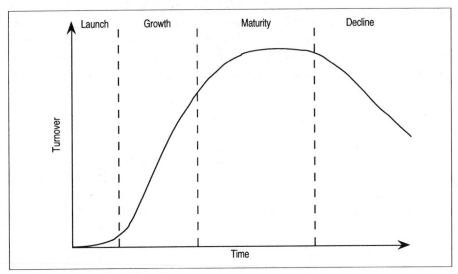

Figure 6.4. The product life cycle.

The length of each phase will depend upon the product and the market. It may also be extended by appropriate marketing action. Probably the best example of that is the car industry where, a few years after its launch, each model tends to receive an uplift or upgrade, in order to extend its life and postpone the need for a completely new model. Does this simple concept have potential value for planning in the public sector?

The origins of the concept are certainly in the private sector, and there may well be doubts as to whether many of the services offered by the public sector are subject to the same pressures of changes in fashion, technology and competition. It is also doubtful whether the concept is particularly helpful when looking at a single product anyway. If we have, for a few years, clearly been in the growth phase, we need to know when we shall move from growth to maturity. However, nothing in the basic concept dictates how long each phase is likely to last. Forecasting turning points takes us back to the problems of the time series and econometric models discussed in the previous chapter and the need to turn to judgemental approaches to forecasting.

Life cycle analysis is more likely to be helpful where an organisation:

- has a wide range of individual products or services
- has some freedom to choose what those products or services should be.

It can then be used as a type of product portfolio analysis, as illustrated in Figure 6.5. Each product or service can be plotted on the generic curve, each one represented by a circle, the magnitude of which is related to turnover. Precision is not vital, so the inability to predict *exactly* how close each product is to a turning point is not overly important. The question to ask is whether the picture presented gives reasonable assurance as to the future, remembering that the circle associated with a particular product ought to grow larger as it moves through the growth phase.

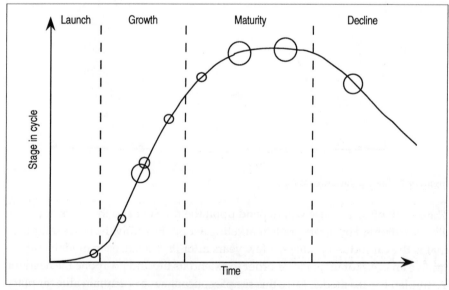

Figure 6.5. Portfolio analysis using the product life cycle.

The pattern shown in Figure 6.5 would raise a few questions:

- given that some new products will fail, is there enough at the launch stage
- even recognising that turnover of a particular product will tend to grow as it moves through the growth stage, is the turnover from the products in that stage sufficient to replace those moving from maturity to decline
- why is the turnover from some of the products in the later part of the growth stage still so small?

Thinking these questions through would help to establish whether there are any problems which need to be addressed.

Value chain analysis

The concept of the value chain was introduced by Porter (1985) in his book on *Competitive Advantage*. The value chain represented a way of looking at a firm's activities to enable it to identify sources of competitive advantage (which is discussed in Chapter 7). Porter's generic model is illustrated in Figure 6.6.

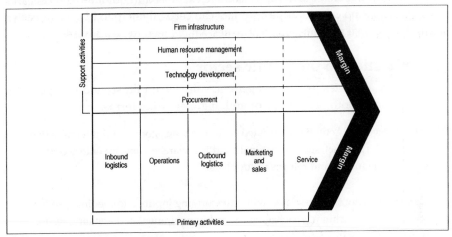

Figure 6.6. Porter's generic value chain.

Reprinted with the permission of The Free Press, a Division of Simon & Schuster from COMPETITIVE ADVANTAGE: Creating and Sustaining Superior Performance by Michael E. Porter. Copyright © 1985 by Michael E. Porter.

❏ The key principles

Activities are divided into two categories, primary and support, the primary activities being those directly related to the production of the product and its provision to the customer. The support activities are those which are necessary to allow the production process to proceed but not directly part of that process.

Key thoughts which seem to lie behind the concept of the value chain are:

- a concentration on activities, successfully adding value, not on functional responsibilities
- the idea of a chain, recognition that activities are linked; for example, the quality of components purchased has implications for the cost of the post delivery service support to the customer
- the consideration of how an activity adds value for the final customer.

It would be ideal if it were possible to link to each activity both a cost and a value. This would enable the firm to ensure that all of its activities were contributing adequately to its profits. It would also be able to compare the costs of its activities with the cost of other companies undertaking similar activities and thereby identify where better cost performance should be feasible. In practice, the data may not be available or obtainable to achieve all this with any precision. This does not detract, though, from the potential value of the thinking process inherent in pursuing the key thoughts listed above. Undertaking the analysis even where the value of activities has to be expressed in qualitative terms and where there are no comparative cost data can certainly help to identify areas of strength and weakness and suggest issues which need to be addressed.

❏ Application to the public sector

The primary activities in Porter's generic value chain illustrated in Figure 6.6 are expressed in both private sector and manufacturing terms:

Inbound logistics. Activities associated with receiving, storing and disseminating inputs to the product, such as material handling, warehousing, inventory control, vehicle scheduling, and returns to suppliers.

Operations. Activities associated with transforming inputs into the final product form, such as machining, packaging, assembly, equipment maintenance, testing, printing, and facility operations.

Outbound logistics. Activities associated with collecting, storing, and physically distributing the product to buyers, such as finished goods warehousing, material handling, delivery vehicle operation, order processing, and scheduling.

Marketing and sales. Activities associated with providing a means by which buyers can purchase the product and inducing them to do so, such as advertising, promotion, sales force, quoting, channel selection, channel relations, and pricing.

Service. Activities associated with providing service to enhance or maintain the value of the product, such as installation, repair, training, parts supply, and product adjustment.

Each of the main five activities is thus broken down into a larger number of separate activities. The actual activities, though, will depend both upon the products being produced and upon the way in which a particular firm is organised. Therefore any firm wishing to construct its value chain cannot turn to a standard code, it has put a good deal of analytical effort into producing a chain appropriate to its own situation. There is no reason why the basic thinking processes should not be applied in a similar way to public sector service activities.

Taking a residential training establishment the activities might be:

- design of course programme
- design of individual courses
- preparation of materials
- booking procedures
- publicity and information
- provision of teaching accommodation
- provision of residential accommodation
- provision of catering
- administrative support to course participants
- library and research facilities
- the teaching
- support materials
- post-course advice.

Alternatively, in the case of payment of some cash benefits activities might include:

- general publicity on the availability of benefits
- provision of literature on how to claim
- person-to-person advice
- accommodation for personal visits
- payments
- anti-fraud activities
- reports on performance.

In this case, the 'added value' is not for the recipients of benefits alone but for a wider group of stakeholders, including the taxpayer in general and Parliament.

The above illustrations are just first thoughts, sufficient, it is hoped, to suggest that value chain thinking can be applied to service activities and to the public sector. Where a service is paid for, it may be possible to put some money values on the 'margin' or 'value added', but in most cases the 'value' would have to be expressed in qualitative terms. It ought to be possible, however, to cost the activities, to allow some cost comparisons with similar activities undertaken by other providers and to permit qualitative assessments of costs against value. The cost comparisons are, in effect, one element of benchmarking which has been discussed earlier.

The 7-S framework

The McKinsey 7-S framework is an example of a checklist technique. The underlying thought is that, for the successful implementation of strategy, there must be a match of the seven elements shown in Figure 6.7. This framework may be used initially to look at the organisation's present position, to help to identify problems and weaknesses which need to be addressed. It can also be used, as strategy is developed, to check that new gaps are not appearing.

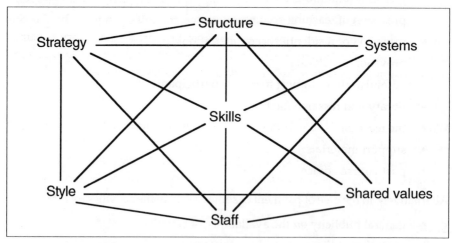

Figure 6.7. The 7-S framework.

❏ Definitions of the Ss

Each of the Ss could be considered independently, each clearly needs to be addressed in the analysis stages of the strategic management process, but the main question to be addressed is whether there is consistency between the different elements. Before thinking a little more about that, however, let us consider what each element covers.

Skills

Skills lie at the centre; the organisation has certain expertise and experience, both in terms of individual members of staff and corporately. There will be certain things which it is good at, it may be scientific or expert knowledge, it may be managing projects, it may be disseminating written information. The word 'skills' places emphasis on the human aspects, but it might be worthwhile to consider including other aspects of capability, such as physical resources and equipment at the organisation's disposal.

Structure

Structure will start with the organisation chart. What is the hierarchy, who is responsible for what, what are the levels of delegation? Is the organisation structured on a regional basis, a functional basis, or on the basis of customer groupings? How does the organisation interface with customers and suppliers? What is the relationship between support groups (eg personnel, finance) and the product or service delivery groups? Ultimately, where does power lie?

Systems

Systems can be formal and informal. Here the concern is with how work processes are organised, how work flows. Who receives the initial enquiry, how is this converted to an order, who processes the order, how are the necessary resources mobilised and the production arranged, how is the product or service delivered to the customers, and how are any costs and revenues accounted for?

Shared values

What does the organisation stand for? The values can have both an external and an internal dimension and can be either formally stated or simply implied. At this stage both negative and positive elements need to be recorded. What appears to be tight management internally might be interpreted as hopelessly bureaucratic by an outside observer.

Staff

This can overlap a little with skills, if the latter embrace individual as well as corporate skills. In looking at the staff, consideration should be given to demography, their experience, training and education, the type of people they are, what they are looking for from their work.

Style

Looking at the way management behaves, at appraisal and reward systems, what type of behaviour is encouraged? What sort of thing is praised, which type of people get promoted? Some of this may be formal (e.g. the annual staff appraisal form), some may be informal. It is important here to ensure an accurate picture of perceptions throughout the organisation, not simply to write down the management team's official stance!

Strategy

What are the current goals, in which direction is the organisation trying to move, which areas is it trying to expand or contract, which skills and behaviour is it trying to encourage?

❑ Using the framework

Having gone through each of the headings in turn and described the situation, the key element of the analysis is to look for inconsistencies between them. A few simple possibilities might be a mismatch between:

- declared values and recent promotions
- direction of change (more rapid response to the customer) and structure (who controls the resources)
- systems (more responsibilities for individuals) and staff knowledge (their experience is restricted to one aspect of the production process)
- areas of growth in demand and the skills and experience of the organisation.

These mismatches identify areas of weakness which need to be addressed in the new plan.

The emphasis above has been on applying the 7-S framework to the existing situation. However, as a new strategy or new business plan develops, the 7-S framework can also be used as an appraisal tool. Applying it to the new plan, is it possible to identify inconsistencies or mismatches which remain? If there are, do action plans exist to put them right?

The 7-S framework is a checklist, a framework for structured discussion. It is unlikely to be used to full advantage if the discussion is confined to the management team. Who is in the best position to say whether style fits with the espoused values? Who is best placed to identify inconsistencies between systems and structures? These questions point to the need to involve a good cross-section of the organisation's staff in the discussion, in focus groups (see Chapter 5) and in a format where they are at ease and do not feel reluctant to reveal their true feelings. More is said about this aspect of organising group discussions under the heading of SWOT analysis in Chapter 7. As a final point, there may also be benefit in consulting outside parties on some aspects of the analysis, for example, the values as they appear to those for whom the service is provided.

Other techniques for internal analysis

Market research was covered in Chapter 5, with the emphasis on research on trends in the external environment. However, market research can also play an important part in the internal analysis, in helping to establish which aspects of an organisation's performance are seen as strong or weak by stakeholders. At its simplest, market research in this context could be some very simple questionnaires given to those who receive the service.

The market research will get more complex when it is necessary to consider attitudes among the wider public or reasons why some people are not using the service offered. Why do some people not claim benefits to which they are entitled? If everybody using our service is well satisfied, why do so many people not use it at all? How does one choose the appropriate sample to answer these questions? How should we frame the questions to obtain answers which can be categorised and analysed? These issues need careful thought and some professional expertise.

When using the techniques considered in this chapter, there will often be a desire to achieve a degree of consensus about the most important points. In such situations, Delphi techniques discussed in Chapter 5 could have a contribution to make.

References

Department of Trade and Industry (1992) *Best Practice in Benchmarking* London, Department of Trade and Industry

Henderson, B. (1984) *The Logic of Business Strategy* Cambridge Mass. Ballinger Publishing Company

Karlöf, B. and Östblom, S. (1993) *Benchmarking: A Signpost to Excellence in Quality and Productivity* Chichester, John Wiley & Sons

Porter, M. E. (1985) *Competitive Advantage: Creating and Sustaining Superior Performance* New York, The Free Press

Chapter 7

Identifying issues

In the previous two chapters, techniques for external and internal analysis have been examined. The purpose of this analysis, following the sequence of the strategic management process described in Chapter 3, was to identify the key issues which the organisation needs to address, the things which the organisation really needs to get right if it is to be successful in fulfilling its basic purpose. The external analysis may itself identify some of these issues, so may the internal analysis. However, very often it is when the external and internal are brought together that the big issues emerge. For example, the areas of activity where demand is likely to grow may be precisely those where our skills and expertise are currently weak. Or maybe the type of service which people are now demanding does not fit with the culture of our staff who prefer certainty.

In this chapter we look at some techniques which bring the external and internal analysis together or which tend in themselves to suggest key issues or to point to the directions which strategies should follow. The particular techniques described are:

- portfolio models
- gap analysis
- competitive advantage
- SWOT analysis.

The chapter concludes with some thoughts on actually identifying the issues and taking them forward.

Portfolio models

The Boston portfolio model described in Chapter 6 was an example of a portfolio model, but one that looked at the dimensions of market share and growth rate, concentrating on the cash generating capability of the range of products. There are other portfolio models where, of the two dimensions considered, one relates to the requirements of the market and the other to the internal capability. The implication is that there is a strategic issue if the market demand is for something where our capability is weak, or vice versa.

Portfolio models were designed primarily for large corporate companies, who needed to consider whether their 'portfolio' of Strategic Business Units (SBUs) was in some sense optimal. The model would form a basis for decisions on acquisition and divestment and on which SBUs should be encouraged to grow. The models can equally be applied to organisations who offer a range of products, to guide decisions on the product portfolio rather than on the SBU portfolio. The basis of the model is simply a matrix with two axes, each defined by one factor. Each SBU or product is defined in terms of the two factors and plotted on the matrix as illustrated in Figure 6.3 in the previous chapter.

❑ Popular portfolio models

The most popular portfolio model which combines external and internal elements is that known as General Electric's planning grid (Hofer and Schendel, 1978). The two dimensions are:

* industry attractiveness
* business strength.

Each is split into three levels, to give a 3 x 3, nine cell, matrix. Industry attractiveness is high, medium or low, business strength is strong, average or weak. Industry attractiveness embraces criteria such as market size, growth rate, barriers to entry, capital requirements, level of competition, seasonality and cyclicality. Business strength reflects the ability to compete on price and quality, knowledge of the market, technological and management capability.

It is also quite common to incorporate life cycle analysis into a portfolio model. The Arthur D Little matrix (Naylor, 1979) plots competitive position against industry maturity. This is a 5 x 4 matrix, with five categories of competitive position, from weak to dominant, and four categories of industry maturity, from embryonic to ageing.

❑ Public sector applications

There is no reason why portfolio models should not be applied to the public sector, though the dimensions of the axes in the most popular private sector models may not be applicable. There is always a need to match capability with the service required, even if these cannot be expressed in terms of competitive strength and market size. However, dimensions such as skills and ability to meet the public's expectations and the public demand could be relevant.

In the private sector, a mismatch between the external attractiveness and internal strength can be addressed either by withdrawal or by strengthening the weak area. In the public sector the choice may be more limited. If a service is part of the mandate, withdrawal is not an option, but the analysis is still valuable in helping to identify the weakness which needs to be addressed.

One other point to bear in mind is that the analysis should not be confined to the present position. The strategic issue is more likely to emerge as a mismatch between our present capability and the service likely to be required in the future, a gap which needs to be bridged.

Gap analysis

The general principle of gap analysis is most easily illustrated by a simple private sector example. The gap analysis starts with three components:

- where we are now
- where we wish to be in a specified future year
- where we will be in that future year on the basis of current strategies.

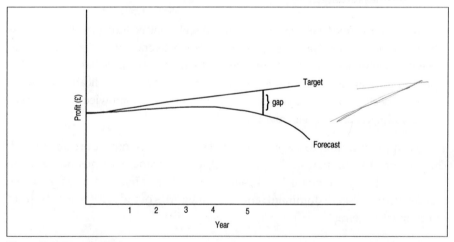

Figure 7.1. Gap analysis.

Figure 7.1 illustrates this, with reference to a profit target. Assuming a planning horizon of five years, the gap is the difference between the target profit for year 5 and the forecast profit for year 5. The issue is then how to close that gap.

❏ The prerequisites of gap analysis

The first requirement for undertaking a gap analysis is a clear view of where we want to be at a particular point of time in the future. It also seems helpful to be able to express the target in numerical terms. According to Argenti (1993), the:

> gap analysis technique is not limited to companies, although it is confined, naturally, to organizations that can quantify their aims.

The view which we have taken is that the aims and core objectives are only in draft form at the early stages of the strategic planning process and are then firmed up as strategic planning proceeds. Certainly we expect numerical targets to emerge but as an output from rather than as an early input to the planning. The situation may be different in the private sector where particular levels of profit, in terms of returns on capital, are a pre-requisite for continuing to attract funding. Nevertheless it has already been noted that a draft aim and core objectives are necessary before external and internal analysis can start. The concept of a gap, even a qualititative one, between what we would like to be and what we would currently expect to be could be useful in identifying issues to be addressed.

A further point to make is that a gap can be closed either by strategies to raise the forecast or by agreement to reduce the target, as recognised by Goodstein, Nolan and Pfeiffer (1992), though they defined the gap as from the current position, not from the forecast position:

> Gap analysis is a time for careful, considered decision making. If the gap between the current state and desired state seems too large to close, then either the desired future must be redefined ... or creative solutions for closing the gap must be developed ... The mission statement may also have to be modified in the process.

❑ Application in the public sector

Argenti (1993) who is a strong advocate of the value of gap analysis has expressed doubts about whether non-profit organisations (NPOs) are ready for gap analysis:

> I have suggested that one of the key distinctions between a company and an NPO lies in their ability to quantify their aims but, in fact, the distinction really lies in their ability to perform this gap analysis calculation. Companies know when they have devised a suitable set of strategies because 'suitable' means 'capable of closing the gap', until NPOs can make this extraordinarily helpful test they will remain second-class organizations. Companies can make such assertions as: 'To hit our targets we need to introduce a new product yielding $20m profits in year 3' or whatever - incredibly valuable revelations. Without the ability to make statements of this sort I question whether the word 'management' means anything at all in the modern, numerate, world.

If we were to accept these strictures completely, there is still one way in which gap analysis can be used within the public sector. The first step is to identify what the organisation would like to be, the volume and quality of service which it feels it should provide. Then, on the basis of its current strategies, it can calculate what level of public funding would be necessary to deliver that service. The next step is to forecast what level of public funding is likely to be available, given the pressures to constrain public expenditure and the competing demands on the funds available. (This would undoubtedly require a major element of judgemental forecasting.) This leaves a gap, and strategies must be formulated to close it, involving, perhaps, combinations of:

- improving efficiency
- reducing service aspirations
- seeking other sources of funding
- bidding more strongly for public funding.

Which of these is feasible will depend upon the particular circumstances, including the mandates, of the organisation.

This sort of approach can be very useful in some of the fundamental expenditure reviews undertaken in relation to the public expenditure survey. For example, what will be the bill for pensions, social security, the health service, the prison service, if current policies are continued? How does this differ from the present bill and from what we think we could afford in the future? How can the gap be closed?

In the writer's view it is also possible to use the general idea of gap analysis to help to identify issues, even where it is less easy to quantify outputs, though the clearer the quantification the more useful gap analysis is likely to be. Such clarity is more likely in the business planning than in the strategic planning cycle. When preparing a new strategy, the aims and objectives emerge as an output from the process. In the case of a business plan, however, the aims and objectives from the strategy represent a given starting point, and the analysis stage of the business planning process will concentrate on comparing actual performance with what had been intended. This seems a good setting for gap analysis.

Competitive advantage

The notion of 'competitive advantage', which now features in most major works on strategy, was expounded by Porter (1980, 1985) in a primarily private sector context. It is an example of an approach which brings both external and internal factors together and, going further than helping to identify issues, suggests what the key features of strategy ought to be. Porter's concern was profitability, and this, he argued, depended heavily on the structure of the industry in which a firm was operating and on the firm's own positioning within that industry (Porter, 1985):

> Industry structure then determines who keeps what proportion of the value a product creates for buyers.

> Positioning determines whether a firm's profitability is above or below the industry average. A firm that can position itself well may earn high rates of return even though industry structure is unfavourable and the average profitability of the industry is therefore modest. The fundamental basis of above-average performance in the long run is *sustainable competitive advantage*.

❏ The five forces

The starting point is an analysis of the industry structure, which Porter presents in terms of five forces, as illustrated in Figure 7.2. This can be used, in itself, as a technique for external analysis, to help identify issues associated with the external environment in which a firm is operating.

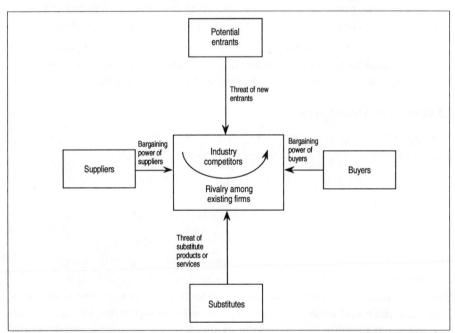

Figure 7.2. Porter's five competitive forces that determine industry profitability.

The five forces seem basically self-explanatory. Although formulated in a private sector context, they seem perfectly applicable to the public sector environment as well:

- *industry competitors* - many public sector organisations are open to competition, for some of their services at least, for example, Her Majesty's Stationery Office, Ordnance Survey, the Civil Service College, or any group which is being or has been market tested
- *potential entrants* - every part of the public sector is being opened as widely as possible to competition, parts of organisations if not whole organisations
- *substitutes* - with the pressures on public expenditure there must be a constant search for alternative ways of providing particular services, including, in the fundamental expenditure reviews, consideration of whether things have to be done at all
- *suppliers* - the public sector buys many billions of pounds worth of supplies and services each year, and if these suppliers are powerful they will have an impact on our ability to control the cost of public services; major defence contracts spring to mind, but remember that the workforce is also a major supplier, of labour, in this context
- *buyers* - in most cases, public services do not have direct buyers, the equivalent force in the public sector is indirectly the taxpayer and more directly the resulting pressures to hold down public expenditure.

❏ Generic strategies

Moving on from the five forces, Porter (1985) proceeds to conclude that, to maintain competitive advantage, there are three generic strategies:

- cost leadership
- differentiation
- focus.

The first two terms are fairly self-explanatory, but are clearly designed for a competitive industry. Basically one needs to be able to produce at lower costs than the competition or to be able to offer a product which is in some way distinguishable from and more attractive than those of competitors. One can either aim for cost leadership or differentiation over a broad range of segments or decide to concentrate on a narrower segment, which is the third generic strategy, 'focus'. The 'focus' strategy can still be sub-divided into an emphasis on either cost leadership or differentiation.

❑ Public sector implications

Clearly the original thinking behind these strategies and the terminology used has a strong private sector feel to it. In the public sector, the options available might be significantly restricted by the mandates, as discussed in Chapter 4. This is particularly so as regards differentiation. There may be strong equity reasons why everyone should be entitled to the same service, and if we are a 'monopoly' supplier of the service we cannot withdraw one particular standard of service without proper political authority. Nevertheless we should be thinking about differentiation in the sense of whether we could offer higher value by offering a wider choice of service, such as, for example, driving tests in the evenings or weekends, at a higher price. Questions of cost leadership and focus in the public sector take us right to questions of which services we should provide, which of those we should provide directly and which should be bought in from other providers.

SWOT analysis

Of all the planning techniques described in this book, SWOT analysis is likely to be the one most familiar to the largest number of people. It is extremely straightforward, a checklist approach, designed to ensure that ideas are generated and brought together under some specific headings which have been found to be helpful in identifying issues. The headings are:

S trengths

W eaknesses

O pportunities

T hreats.

Strengths and weaknesses involve looking internally at the organisation, opportunities and threats focus on trends and likely developments in the external environment.

The simplicity and familiarity of the approach may serve to undermine its value in some people's eyes. Here it is suggested that it should be used at the point when issues have to be identified. At this stage the results obtained by using other techniques can be incorporated into the SWOT analysis.

❑ Some principles of SWOT analysis

The first issue is, who should be involved? There are dangers in restricting the

SWOT analysis to the management team. These are:

- a narrow perspective, they may not be very close, for example, to problems at the 'sharp end' which are affecting service delivery
- there may be an implicit wish to justify the strategies already being pursued
- the analysis is not owned in any way by a wider group of staff.

It is therefore strongly recommended that SWOT analysis should be combined with the idea of focus groups. The writer has found it very helpful to undertake the SWOT analysis in three stages:

- in focus groups
- with the management team
- then, to show the management team the results from the focus groups and make a comparison with their own.

If there are significant differences between the two, and there usually are, that suggests an issue in its own right.

Strengths and weaknesses are meant to be internal, opportunities and threats to be external. In practice people sometimes find it difficult to distinguish between strengths and opportunities (eg engineering expertise which could be used to expand the range of services) and between weaknesses and threats (eg our inability to recruit.) Time should not be spent worrying about such boundary disputes. The purpose of the categories is to ensure that each category is given adequate attention. As long as something is identified and recorded, it does not really matter where it sits.

There are frequently potential disputes as to whether a particular point constitutes a strength or a weakness. Staff commitment is a good example. On the one hand, loyalty and hard work are good, but the commitment to what people are currently doing could be a barrier to change. The SWOT analysis is not really the stage to resolve this. Instead, write it down as both a strength and a weakness, which clearly marks it out as an issue to be identified and addressed at the next stage of the planning.

A SWOT analysis should basically take a brainstorming approach. The desire is to identify a large number of ideas, initially at least. It is important not to let people get away with suggestions that 'the building' is a weakness. What is it about the building? In the early stages of the SWOT analysis, we should be anxious to find out all the aspects of the building which worry people, poor temperature control, lack of natural daylight, shabby office furniture, too far to the toilets, lack of storage space, and so on. At a later stage it is worth trying to group the points under higher level headings, but when these are carried forward to the next stages in the planning process the detail can be extremely helpful. For example, when generating options for dealing with the 'building' issue and when appraising those options, it is helpful to refer back to the detailed points. Bryson (1988) suggests a snow-card approach to generate the ideas and group them together. Self-adhesive note pads are also an extremely helpful aid; if people place their initial thoughts on these notes, it is easy to move the notes around later to group them under higher level headings.

❏ Conducting the exercise

As with any group technique, it is important to ensure that the process is not dominated by one or two strong individuals. To that end it is sometimes worth asking individuals to write down all their own ideas first and contribute them anonymously to the pool. The group would then bring them together under higher level headings and remove duplicates. Another option is to put sheets of paper on the wall, under each of the four SWOT headings and ask people to write their ideas on adhesive notes and attach them to the paper.

There is a risk, as in any brainstorming exercise, that people will flag before too long. It is actually very difficult to brainstorm for long enough to complete each of the four categories in turn. If the exercise is conducted in that way, it is wise to start with opportunities and threats while people are fresh; they tend to find these more difficult than strengths and weaknesses. However, an alternative is to divide the group into four, ask each sub-group to brainstorm one of the headings, then pass the results round to the other sub-groups and ask them to add further ideas.

A final point to consider is the importance of reflecting the future, not just the present. If the external analysis earlier has revealed the likelihood of having to operate in different ways, what is a strength now could be a weakness if one is looking three years ahead. Whoever is facilitating the SWOT analysis will need to draw this to the attention of those participating.

Identifying the issues

From all the analysis now undertaken, from the results obtained by whichever techniques have been used, how does one identify the issues? At this point, there are no new techniques to employ. We have to review the information gathered, apply brainpower, and seek to identify, in the words of Figure 3.2, the things:

we must really do something about if we are to be successful.

Bryson (1988) defines a strategic issue as a:

fundamental policy choice affecting an organization's mandates, mission, values, product or service level and mix, clients or users, cost, financing, organization or management.

That seems an excellent definition for the strategic planning cycle. In the business planning cycle the issues are likely to be associated more with gaps between what the strategy demanded and what has actually been achieved so far. They are less likely to involve mandates and missions, but could well arise in any of the other areas mentioned by Bryson.

The most important practical point about this stage is not to rush it. People do need to review carefully the information which has been collected and what it means, not simply come up with the things which they had always felt needed addressing. There could well be benefit in:

- giving people some time to absorb the information
- forcing every key individual to think seriously about it by writing something down
- requiring the written ideas to be backed up by argumentation, as to why the issues suggested are key ones
- subjecting everyone's ideas to scrutiny and debate.

So what sort of argumentation should be looked for, to identify something as a key issue? Firstly it, should be possible to point to elements of the analysis where it emerged. Secondly, it should be possible to relate it to the topics contained in the quotation above from Bryson. Thirdly, it should be possible to point to real options, choices which have to be made; at this stage preferences for particular options should not be expressed, but some examples of the range of choice would help.

The key issues may have emerged from one piece of analysis alone, for example, one major stakeholder is dissatisfied, or there are too few products in the growth stage. Others will emerge by putting different elements of analysis together, for example a combination of a weakness and a threat, or a whole series of questions from market research, benchmarking, value chains, SWOT about the cost and quality of a particular administrative process. They need to be fundamental. Going back to what was said under the heading of SWOT analysis, the issue now is 'the building,' not the individual elements of the building which we wanted people to concentrate on when suggesting weaknesses. However, it is suggested that each issue should be described on about a page of paper, explaining why it is an issue, how the issue emerged, and some of the detailed points made about it. This will be valuable when moving on to identify options and appraise them.

A final point is that, if issues appear to emerge in the early stages of analysis, it is probably worth recording them at that stage. They can then be brought forward for further consideration at the current stage, for integration with other issues, amendment in the light of subsequent information, or even rejection as no longer an issue or no longer an issue of sufficient importance.

References

Argenti, J. (1993) *Your Organisation: What is it for?* Maidenhead, McGraw-Hill

Bryson, J. (1988) *Strategic Planning for Public and Nonprofit Organizations* London, Jossey-Bass

Goldstein, L. D. Nolan, T.M. and Pfeiffer, J. W. (1992) *Applied Strategic Planning: A Comprehensive Guide* San Diego, Pfeiffer and Company

Hofer, C. and Schendel, D. (1978) *Strategy Formulation: Analytical Concepts* St Paul MN, West Publishing Company

Naylor, T. H. (1979) *Corporate Planning Models* Reading MA, Addison-Wesley

Porter, M. E. (1980) *Competitive Strategy: Techniques for Analyzing Industries and Competitors* New York, The Free Press

Porter, M. E. (1985) *Competitive Advantage: Creating and Sustaining Superior Performance* New York, The Free Press

Chapter 8

Investigating options

A key feature of an issue is that it gives rise to options. As explained in Chapter 3, the nature and style of the options can differ considerably from one issue to another. There can also be a difference between the strategic plan and the business plan in the extent to which some issues need to be resolved immediately. At one extreme there can be issues which clearly require further investigation, but this investigation can be left to the business plan. They might appear in the business plan as an objective to:

> complete a review and present recommendations to the Board by ... (a specified date).

The main choice in the strategic plan is then which of the issues need to be studied first, which have the highest priority? It is much less likely that issues can be left like that in the business planning process, though there may be some cases where completion of the study can be made a target in the one-year plan.

There may be other issues where, on reflection, the objective is clear and responsibility for decisions on how to achieve the objective can be delegated, left to the responsible manager. This situation may be more likely in the business planning than in the strategic planning process.

Other issues will need careful investigation and high-level decision before the plan can be finalised. This might be done in a number of ways:

- careful consideration by the management team
- investigation and data collection by the planners or some other group, feeding the information back to the management team for decision
- investigation by a project team, who bring recommendations back to the management team for approval.

Hopefully the above is sufficient to show that there are many different ways to take issues forward. The important thing is that those leading the planning process should consider *each* issue on its merits and make a firm decision as to the next action required. Issues must not just be left hanging in the air. It is also clear that someone is going to need to look at and decide between options. In this chapter we look at the techniques which can be used to generate the options and appraise them.

Generating options

It is, of course, a truism that no final decision can be better than the options identified; hence the importance of encouraging ideas, some radical thinking, about what *might* be done. Yet this is an area of planning which receives remarkably little attention. It is only too easy to confine the thinking to things which people have always really wanted to do, pet ideas from the recent past, rather than thinking of quite different approaches. Creative thinking has to be encouraged. Here we look at two approaches to creative thinking, as examples.

❑ Brainstorming

There are probably very few people who have had no experience of brainstorming. Nevertheless, or perhaps even because of that, it may be worthwhile to remind ourselves of some of the basic principles of brainstorming

Brainstorming is defined by Rawlinson (1986) as:

> a means of getting a large number of ideas from a group of people in a short time.

The intention of brainstorming is to generate ideas, not to discuss them or evaluate them, hence the emphasis on a large number in a small time.

Rules for brainstorming

The basic rules for an effective brainstorming session are shown in Figure 8.1. 'No evaluation' is perhaps the primary rule. A major barrier to creativity is fear, fear of being made to look silly, fear of one's standing with colleagues, seniors or juniors. Ideas need to be valued, every idea must be welcomed as a contribution to the later thinking.

In a brainstorming session the thinking is not intended to be structured. Although there is likely to be some element of association, sudden jumps are welcome and indeed are to be encouraged.

Enormity means volume, quantity. This is one area where quantity rules, not quality. Keep the ideas coming, keep recording them.

Finally, kidnap means that it is quite in order to build on another person's idea, to extend it, improve on it, even plagiarise it.

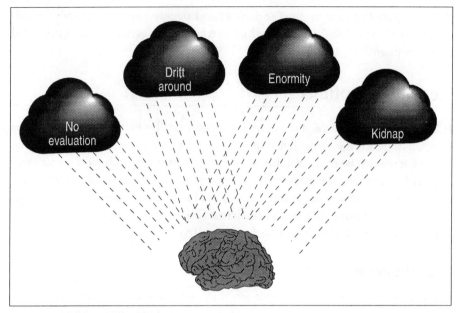

Figure 8.1. Brainstorming rules.

These rules should be made clear at the start of the session, indeed it may be sensible to have them displayed, so that the leader can quickly point them out to an offender, preferably an admonishment administered amidst laughter!

The procedure

How large should the group be? Rawlinson (1986) suggests about 12 and not more than 20. If the group is too large, there are likely to be some people who find it difficult to make themselves heard or who decide to be passengers and not contribute at all. Too small a group, less than six or seven, is unlikely to generate sufficient variety or interaction.

Who should they be? It is important that, with the help of whatever initial briefing is offered, they should feel familiar enough with the issue to be able to offer ideas. Some familiarity is advisable, though too much familiarity can prevent people from ranging widely enough.

The brainstorming session does need some careful preparation. There must be some structure to the exercise even if we do not want the thinking to be structured. The session should start with a statement of the problem, by the facilitator or by the 'owner' of the problem. This should then be discussed, and questions answered, to help to clarify the problem for all the participants. But too much detail should be avoided.

The next step recommended in textbooks is to suggest some restatements of the problem. To be a restatement, it must be capable of being written in the form 'how to ...?' Then one restatement has to be selected and is expressed in the form 'how many ways are there to ...?' An example given by Titman (1990) relates to law centres offering free legal advice to those of low income:

Problem	-	Law centres do not have enough money
Restatements	-	How to reduce costs?
	-	How to increase contributions?
	-	How to find new sources of funds?
	-	How to reduce services?
	-	How to raise funds?
	-	How to get other bodies to take over the work?
Selected restatement	-	In how many ways can a law centre raise funds?

It is always possible to brainstorm another restatement later if desired.

Before moving on to the main brainstorming session, it is sometimes helpful to do a warm-up, for example by choosing a small everyday object and asking how many ways it can be used. Then everyone is prepared for and in the mood to brainstorm the main problem. Remember, every idea is written down and displayed. When the session is finished, which should be when the ideas have dried up, the ideas have to be evaluated. This should not be done immediately. It is better to type all the ideas up first, and then present them as a long list to those who will be participating in appraisal, within a few days. Those who brainstormed can also be asked to undertake the appraisal. Approaches to appraisal are described later in this chapter.

❏ Fish-boning

As can be imagined, brainstorming is particularly useful when it is felt that there could be a very large number of possibilities or options. Where the number of options does not appear so large, it may be wise to consider the fish-boning approach, which has the merit of presenting the ideas in a structured form which helps to highlight the key choices and make it easier to decide where the appraisal effort should be concentrated. The fish-boning technique can be used in creative thinking, logical thinking, structuring and making choices.

An example of fish-boning is given in Figure 8.2. (The reason for the name should

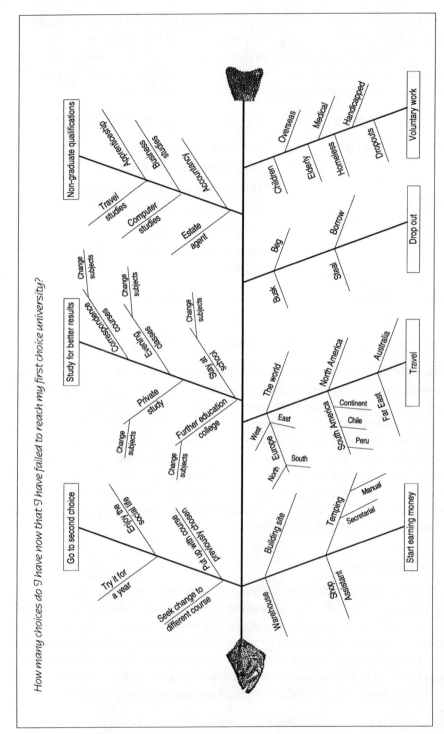

Figure 8.2. Fish-boning.

be reasonably clear!) The starting point is a problem. In this case the problem is that your exam results (at A level) have not been good enough to earn you a place at your first choice university. They are good enough to enable you to go to your second choice but you have now decided that you do not really want to do that course. What options do you have?

It can be seen that each main bone of the fish is associated with a major option written in the box at the end of the bone. Then each smaller bone running off the main bone represents a sub-option within the major one. There are also sub-options to the sub-options! Some people may like to try to fill in the major options first, others may prefer to identify the more detailed options first and then add the descriptions of the major choices later. Others may prefer to brainstorm and then use the fish-bone to sort the ideas later.

Appraising the options

Once the options have been generated, the next step is to decide what choices need to be made. This is by no means as straightforward as it appears. If a good number of ideas has been generated, there will be insufficient time to consider thoroughly all of the choices which could theoretically be possible. Consider first the hierarchy of choice, in Figure 8.3, with examples taken from the fish-bone in Figure 8.2. In a real case there will be a number of separate issues as well, each issue with its own fish-bone.

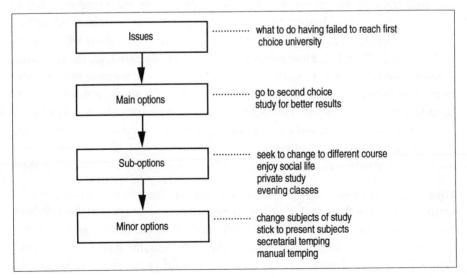

Figure 8.3. The hierarchy of choice.

It would suit those who like to follow structured approaches to do this exercise either bottom-up or top-down. The bottom-up approach would proceed as follows:

1. under each sub-option, choose the best minor option;

2. now that we have cleared up any uncertainty about what the sub-option means, choose the best sub-option under each main option

3. now that we have cleared up the uncertainty about what each main option means, choose between the main options, so that we know which main option we will pursue to resolve each issue.

An alternative structured approach would start from the top down, by choosing between the main options, would then consider the sub-options within that main option, then having chosen a sub-option, would move on to the minor options. The top-down approach involves a good deal less work, because fewer choices are appraised, but it leaves us to try to choose between ill-defined options; each main option could still take us in quite different directions, depending upon which sub-options are selected.

In reality, it will not be possible to follow such a structured pattern of choice. Such a structure assumes that the choices at any level are mutually exclusive, whereas in practice the choice is often not either A or B, but how much of A and how much of B. There will be examples of mutually exclusive choices; if it is chosen to relocate the headquarters operations, ultimately only one choice can be made (though the choice may be to relocate part in one place and part in another). More often, though, the question will be how to distribute effort and resources. Perhaps we have identified that we need to improve our level of service in areas A, B and C. How should our efforts be allocated, all to A, equally between the three, 60% to C, 30% to A and 10% to B? Choosing between the issues will certainly need to be considered that way. We would not wish to concentrate solely on one issue. We could decide that we have to leave some issues on one side for now, but our choices will concentrate on establishing priorities. Similarly when choosing between main options, we may well end up deciding to pursue four sub-options from one, two from another and none from another.

The complexity of the above explains why careful thought should be given to sorting out where the effort of option appraisal should be concentrated. Where are the key choices which need to be addressed? How should we go about producing the data to inform those choices and about actually making the choices? Which techniques should be used and who should be involved in helping to make those choices?

In the following sections we first explain two main techniques which can, and almost certainly need to, be used to help in making the necessary choices:

- discounted cash flow techniques
- weighting and ranking.

In the context of discounted cash flow techniques, reference is also made to cost–benefit analysis which is appropriate to some strategic issues within the public sector. We then offer a few thoughts on other techniques which can play a part in the appraisal process. Finally, we return to the question of whom to involve in the choice process.

Discounted cash flow techniques

Wherever choices have a financial dimension, it is likely that a first stage in the appraisal process should be some discounted cash flow analysis. To illustrate why such analysis is necessary, it may be helpful to identify the somewhat rare circumstances under which it is not necessary.

The need for discounted cash flow analysis arises because a pound today does not have the same value as a pound in a year's time, even if there were no inflation. People are not indifferent between offers of

- £100 today, and
- £100, updated to reflect the level of inflation, a year from today.

The reasons for this range from the simple to the complex, but examples are:

- £100 now can be invested and be worth more than £100 plus inflation in a year's time
- there is a risk that I might die within the year
- I should be a bit better off in a year's time, so the money will not be worth so much to me
- I desperately need some cash now.

If there are two options with the cost streams shown in example 1 in Figure 8.4, none of the considerations listed above will come into play. Option B costs more than option A in each and every year. Whatever the organisation's pressures on cash flow in a particular year, option B is inferior to option A, it is inferior at each and every point.

	Example 1		Example 2		Example 3	
	Cost of option A	Cost of option B	Cost of option A	Cost of option B	Cost of option A	Cost of option B
Year	(£)	(£)	(£)	(£)	(£)	(£)
0	500	700	500	700	500	700
1	70	80	70	80	70	80
2	70	80	70	80	70	80
3	70	80	70	80	70	60
4	90	110	90	80	90	50
5	90	110	90	80	90	40
6	90	110	90	80	90	40
7	50	110	50	80	50	40
8	50	110	50	80	50	40
9	100	110	100	120	100	80
10	20	50	20	50	20	20

Figure 8.4. The need for discounted cash flow analysis.

Example 2 in Figure 8.4 introduces a complication, because option B is now slightly cheaper than option A in years 4, 5 and 6, but it can be seen that such an advantage is hardly likely to offset option B's additional costs in other years. In this situation, full discounted cash flow analysis may not be justified. However, in Example 3, option B is more expensive initially, but from year 3 onwards becomes considerably cheaper? Is it worth spending the extra immediately (in year 0) in order to make the savings later on? In this situation a full discounted cash flow (DCF) analysis is required.

❏ The principles of discounted cash flow

It is not the intention in this short description to provide sufficient detail to enable the reader without any prior knowledge to become an expert in discounted cash flow analysis. Such techniques should be well known to economists and accountants (and to those who have been closely involved with major capital projects), and such experts should be called upon. Here the purpose is to explain the approach in very simple terms, so that readers can appreciate a little more of why the technique can inform decisions.

Comparing cost streams

An organisation has reached the point where it needs to purchase a new item of capital equipment, in order to maintain the service which it has been mandated to provide. For simplicity, in this first set of calculations, we will assume that the equipment will have an infinite life if properly maintained and that these maintenance costs are included in the running costs.

The choice is between:

Item A   -   initial cost of £400,000 and a running cost of £40,000 a year

Item B - initial cost of £200,000 and a running cost of £50,000 a year.

It is assumed that the interest rate is 8%, that is, funds invested can earn 8% a year, and that there is no inflation.

Firstly consider item A. If we were to place a sum of £500,000 in an investment yielding 8% a year, at the end of the first year we would have earned £40,000 in interest. This could be withdrawn, leaving the capital sum of £500,000 intact, to earn £40,000 again the following year, and the process can be repeated year after year. In other words, investing £500,000 in year 0 at 8% allows £40,000 a year to be withdrawn year after year. Thus item A could be funded by spending £900,000 in year 0, representing £400,000 for the initial purchase and £500,000 to invest to meet the running costs in all future years. This figure, the sum which could theoretically fund the purchase and maintenance of the equipment throughout its life, is known as the *present value*.

Turning to item B, the annual running cost is £50,000. To fund this, we would need to invest £625,000, the interest on which, at 8%, would be £50,000 a year. The present value is then £825,000, that sum of £625,000 plus the £200,000 required to buy the equipment initially. Therefore, in terms of present value, or life time cost, item B is more cost-effective than item A.

Cost and benefit streams

Now look at a situation where we have to consider whether to buy an item of new technology which will cost £300,000 to buy, will last ten years and, after allowing for maintenance costs, will save us £40,000 a year. Again assume an interest rate of 8% a year. In effect, the offer is to set aside £300,000 now in order to obtain £40,000 a year for ten years. The question is, how much would we need to set aside, if we were to invest it at 8%, in order to be able to withdraw (obtain a benefit of) £40,000 a year? The answer is, in fact, £268,403.26 which, at 8%, earns interest of £21,472.26 in the first year, raising the amount available to £289,875.52; withdrawing the £40,000 then leaves a sum of £249,875.52 to start the following year. As shown in Figure 8.5, continuing in the same way, the capital sum is just exhausted at the end of ten years.

The sum of £268,403.26 is known as the *present value* of the benefit stream of £40,000 a year for ten years at an interest rate (technically normally termed the discount rate) of 8%. As this present value is less than the cost of the new technology, the implication is that the new technology would not represent good value for money.

Returning now to Example 3, in Figure 8.4, the approach to choosing between options is to calculate the present value of the cost associated with each year,

Year	Figure in account at start of year	Interest added during year	Figure withdrawn at end of year
1	268403.26	21472.26	40000
2	249875.52	19990.04	40000
3	229865.56	18389.25	40000
4	208254.81	16660.39	40000
5	184915.20	14793.22	40000
6	159708.42	12776.67	40000
7	132485.09	10598.81	40000
8	103083.90	8246.71	40000
9	71330.61	5706.45	40000
10	37037.06	2962.96	40000
11	zero		

Figure 8.5. Illustration of meaning of present value.

then add up these figures to calculate a present value for the option as a whole. The present value (PV) for the cost (C) associated with a particular year (n), at a particular interest rate (i, expressed as a decimal, i.e. 8% = 0.08) is:

$$PV = \frac{C}{(I + i)^n}$$

where:

$$\frac{1}{(1 + i)^n}$$

is known as the discount factor. The calculations for Example 3 are shown in Figure 8.6, and indicate that option A is more cost effective than option B.

	Example 3 (from Figure 8.4)					
Year	Option A			Option B		
	Cost	Discount factor (at 8%)	Discounted cost	Cost	Discount factor (at 8%)	Discounted cost
0	500	1	500.00	700	1	700.00
1	70	0.9259	64.81	80	0.9259	74.07
2	70	0.8573	60.01	80	0.8573	68.58
3	70	0.7938	55.57	60	0.7938	47.63
4	90	0.7350	66.15	50	0.7350	36.75
5	90	0.6806	61.25	40	0.6806	27.22
6	90	0.6302	56.72	40	0.6302	25.21
7	50	0.5835	29.18	40	0.5835	23.34
8	50	0.5403	27.02	40	0.5403	21.61
9	100	0.5002	50.02	80	0.5002	40.02
10	20	0.4632	9.26	20	0.4632	9.26
Present value			979.99			1073.69

Figure 8.6. Example of calculation of present value of a cost stream.

It is hoped that the above illustrations serve to indicate the role of discounted cash flow analysis and the underlying principles. Detailed guidance on these techniques is produced by the Treasury (1991), who also issue from time to time further guidance notes on specific appraisal topics, such as property issues or appraising private financing options. The Treasury also stipulate the value of the discount rate to be used in these calculations. At the time of writing the rate is 6% or 8%, depending upon the circumstances. These figures are real rates, that is, rates over and above the rate of general inflation.

❏ Cost–benefit analysis

In introducing the section on discounted cash flow techniques, it was suggested that this analysis should be the first step wherever a choice had a financial dimension. However, most strategic decisions have a non-financial dimension as well, whether in the public or private sectors, and non-financial considerations tend to be an appropriate feature of many public sector issues anyway. The section below, on weighting and ranking techniques, shows how to tackle the non-financial considerations or how to include them alongside the financial. Before moving to the use of those techniques, however, it is worth considering whether any of these non-financial dimensions can, in fact, be expressed in financial terms. This is where cost–benefit analysis fits in.

In a cost–benefit analysis, an attempt is made to place monetary values on the benefits of particular policies, projects or strategies, when those benefits do not produce a flow either of revenue or of cost savings. This situation is likely to arise in the context of policy decisions on whether particular services should be provided at all or on whether they should be enhanced. Cost–benefit analysis has been used to obtain monetary estimates of the benefits of:

- journey time savings from road improvements
- economic savings from reductions in accidents
- value of recreational access to the countryside, eg in publicly owned forests
- benefits of cleaner air
- the economic benefits of education.

There are many more examples as well. Much of this work can be extremely complex and would require the help of specialists. There are also specialist texts on the subject, for example, Walshe and Daffern (1990), for those who may need to get involved with such studies. The main issue for managers is to consider where and when such analysis may be helpful to inform key decisions in the strategic management process.

❏ Weighting and ranking

Weighting and ranking techniques are an aid to structured decision making. They recognise the need for subjectivity, but are designed to encourage people to make those subjective judgements explicit, to think them through as carefully as possible. Decisions on strategy are likely to contain many subjective elements, in which case discounted cash flow analysis will tend to play a relatively minor part, except where major choices as to capital investment projects are at issue. It is quite possible that the financial choices will feature more strongly in business planning, where the allocation of resources is a key element.

Weighting and ranking essentially involves assessing and scoring each of a number of options against each of a number of criteria in turn, then adding up the scores and reviewing the results. The main problem is often determining the criteria to be used.

Choosing the assessment criteria

For any choice which is being made, the starting point is the question, 'what are we trying to achieve?' What are the results which we want? One way of expressing this is to go back to the analysis stage earlier in the process and ask the questions:

- how much does it contribute towards our aims and core objectives
- how far does it build on our strengths
- how far does it go in addressing our weaknesses
- how far does it help us to seize the opportunities which we have identified
- how far does it help us to counter the threats which we have identified?

These could be the criteria themselves, but they are really too wide. Each of these criteria needs to be broken down into smaller components, otherwise the debate on how well the options shape up against each criterion will be too general, too wide-ranging, not specific enough.

Another categorisation which may help to stimulate the generation of criteria is that of:

- suitability
- feasibility
- acceptability.

This is, for instance, used by Johnson and Scholes (1993). The categories are perhaps best illustrated by examples of the criteria which might be chosen from each.

Suitability - fit with our values
- fit with our skills
- fit with our organisation
- fit with our basic purposes
- fit with opportunities identified
- contribution to combatting threats identified
- contribution to overcoming weaknesses identified
- exploitation of the strengths identified

Feasibility - chances of obtaining the capital funds, the necessary money
- chances of obtaining funds for running costs
- financial returns from discounted cash flow analysis
- chances of attaining the quality of service
- chances of beating any competition and combating competitive reactions
- chances of being able to manage the proposed degree of change
- chances of obtaining the inputs required
- chances of obtaining or building any new skills required
- chances of achieving changes in attitudes

Acceptability - acceptability to ministers
- acceptability to recipients of the service
- acceptability to relevant lobby groups
- acceptability to our own staff
- level of any financial risk
- acceptability to other organisations providing related services.

The assessment procedure

The procedure described below is illustrated in Figure 8.7, using some purely hypothetical numbers. The first step is to determine the criteria, as discussed above, and list them, as in the first column of Figure 8.7. The nature of the criteria will clearly be dependent on the nature of the choice under consideration.

The second step is to weight the criteria according to their importance. The easiest approach is to start with the criterion regarded as the least important and give it a weight of one. Then other criteria can then be weighted accordingly.

Decision criterion	Weighting	Unweighted scores			Weighted scores		
		Option A	Option B	Option C	Option A	Option B	Option C
1. Fit with basic purpose	2	5	3	2	10	6	4
2. Fit with our values	2	4	4	2	8	8	4
3. Fit with our skills	1	3	4	3	3	4	3
4. Ease of building new skills	2	1	6	3	2	12	6
5. Results of DCF analysis	2	4	2	4	8	4	8
6. Availability of funds	4	2	3	5	8	12	20
7. Chances of success	4	1	5	4	4	20	16
8. Acceptability to politicians	5	4	1	5	20	5	25
9. Acceptability to service recipients	3	2	6	2	6	18	6
10. Acceptability to staff	2	6	2	2	12	4	4
Total scores		32	36	32	81	93	96

Figure 8.7. Illustration of weighting and ranking.

The third step is to take each criterion in turn and ask which of the options meets that criterion best? The approach taken in Figure 8.7 is to allow ten points for each criterion, and then allocate these points between the options. If wished all ten points could be allocated to one option if it very clearly dominated all of the other options. Or, if there was nothing to choose between the options, the points could be allocated equally (though this is not straightforward with ten points to be shared between three options). If there is a large number of options, it is necessary to allow more points for each criterion, to permit sufficient discrimination between the options.

The fourth step is to multiply the score for each option against each criterion by the weight for that criterion, to obtain the weighted scores. The weighted scores for each option are then added up to obtain the total score, and the option with the highest score is, at this stage, the preferred option. In the example in Figure 8.7, option C scores best, but is only slightly ahead of option B and, given the subjective elements in both the weighting and the scoring, it would have to be said that option A is not far behind.

The fifth step is to look back at the results carefully, and explain why the results have turned out as they have. Then consider, does this make sense? Sensitivity tests are extremely important. Think where the judgements were most difficult or subject to the greatest uncertainty. What would happen to the final results if those judgements were changed? It is often very illuminating to approach the sensitivity tests from the other end. How would we have to change the weightings or the scorings to alter the final ranking of the options? In this way, the procedure of weighting and ranking is a helpful aid to decision making, it does not itself offer a simple or definitive answer.

❏ Other techniques

Finally, in regard to techniques, we look briefly at the role which a few other techniques can play in the appraisal process. Those covered are:

- business models
- scenarios
- portfolio models and the 7-S framework.

Business models

As explained, the weighting and ranking procedure incorporates a good deal of subjective judgement. However, the subjectivity of these judgements may be reduced by undertaking objective analysis wherever possible before embarking on the weighting and ranking. The financial analysis described earlier is a case in point. One of the criteria may be 'financial viability'. That should not be left just to subjective judgement, it should be examined as objectively as possible beforehand. Similarly, the feasibility of achieving particular levels of service could be investigated prior to the weighting and ranking. In investigating such issues it is often helpful to have a business model, a largely numerical model which allows us to investigate, with the help of a computer, the implications of particular events on business performance. Such a model will be based on particular physical and financial relationships, for example:

- an increase in pay of 2%, given that staff costs make up half of our running costs, will increase total running costs by 1%
- an increase in workload of 10% for a month will require either a temporary 5% increase in staffing plus overtime working or will increase average turnround times by 2 days for that month and the following two months.

Models of business relationships of this sort can be extremely helpful in answering straightforward 'what if' questions and can therefore play a role in sensitivity testing and improving understanding of the risks associated with particular assumptions or particular choices.

Scenarios

At the start of this chapter it was explained that there are very often large numbers of potential options. One way to reduce the number is to combine some of the choices to build some scenarios which appear internally consistent. This can be particularly helpful at the strategic level. For example, if it were decided that a major new type of service had to be offered, it may be clear that this would require the recruitment of new skills, retraining of many existing staff, an internal restructuring, some new technology and some new service outlets. That could be one scenario, which could then be compared with other scenarios. The scenarios are then options for appraisal.

When it comes to the level of business planning, the scenario will have already been chosen, and the remaining choices ought to be less complex, for example:

- the balance of recruitment as against retraining
- how much and which new technology
- where the new service outlets should be located
- the form of the new internal structure.

Portfolio analysis and the 7-S framework

Portfolio analysis and the 7-S framework were described earlier, under the heading of techniques for internal analysis. They were being seen there as tools to examine how the organisation stands at present. They could equally be used to draw up views of how the organisation would stand in the future if particular options or strategies were pursued. In one sense they suggest criteria against which options can be appraised. Have we produced a balanced portfolio? Do shared values fit with strategies? Do skills fit with our style and systems?

Who does the appraisal

Some of the techniques described in this chapter do require specialist skills. Managers ought to be aware of the techniques, what they can do, the basic principles of how they work, and how to interpret the results! However, specialists may need to undertake the detailed work. Techniques which come into this category are:

- discounted cash flow techniques
- cost–benefit analysis
- business modelling.

These specialists will, however, need to involve those staff who are close to the action to provide vital data and to help to build the key relationships in any modelling work. Specialists, operators and managers will need to work closely together, to help to produce results which people understand and in which they have confidence.

The weighting and ranking technique lends itself to wide involvement. When judgements have to be made, it is wise to call upon a wide range of experience, though the management team ultimately has to make the final decision. The exercise could be undertaken by different groups of staff and the results compared. This comparison is often illuminating for top management (and can serve to highlight some of the strategic issues which they face, such as wide differences of view within the organisation). The exercise can also be undertaken by a number of individuals and it is possible to give instant feedback, following a Delphi approach, if each person feeds their results into a computer.

There is one technical point where different individuals or groups undertake the exercise and where the wish is to compare results. If one group allocates weights which tend to be higher on average than another group, the first group's weighted scores will automatically be higher than the second group's. Adding the scores of the two groups together would, in effect, place greater weight on the first group's opinions. If the exercise is approached in this way, each group should be given the same fixed number of points to allocate between the criteria.

References

Johnson, G. and Scholes, K. (1993) *Exploring Corporate Strategy* Hemel Hempstead, Prentice-Hall

Rawlinson, J. G. (1986) *Creative Thinking and Brainstorming* Aldershot, Wildwood House

Titman, L. G. (1990) *The Executive Office: A Handbook of Modern Office Management* London, Cassell

HM Treasury (1991) *Economic Appraisal in Central Government: A Technical Guide for Government Departments* London, HMSO

Walshe, G. and Daffern, P. (1990) *Managing Cost Benefit Analysis* Basingstoke, MacMillan

Chapter 9

Aims, objectives and action plans

The concept of action, of making desired things happen, is a key element of strategic management. As explained in the opening chapters, a common problem with planning has been that plans, once completed, sit on shelves, and the planning process appears divorced from the regular management of the organisation. This is not the type of planning which we wish to encourage, hence the third of the three As described earlier, action.

In Chapter 3, emphasis was placed on the role of aims, objectives and targets rather than on action plans per se in ensuring action. This is in the spirit of empowerment and delegation, making clear to people what outputs or outcomes are expected from them, and then leaving them a good deal of freedom to determine exactly how those results are to be brought about. The need for action plans must not be forgotten and we will return to that, but this chapter starts with a description and explanation of the Sunningdale model, which is designed to ensure that aims, objectives and targets are coherent and consistent throughout an organisation and that responsibilities are clear. There is then an explanation of what makes a good objective and of the qualities of performance indicators which are required in order to set targets. We then turn briefly to action planning and to some approaches which come into the category of techniques to deliver results:

- project management
- total quality management
- business process re-engineering.

The Sunningdale model

The starting point for the Sunningdale model, illustrated in Figure 9.1, is the assumption that the analysis and appraisal stages of the strategic management process have been completed. Choices have been made. It is known which initiatives will be pursued. Now we have to ensure that our intentions are realised.

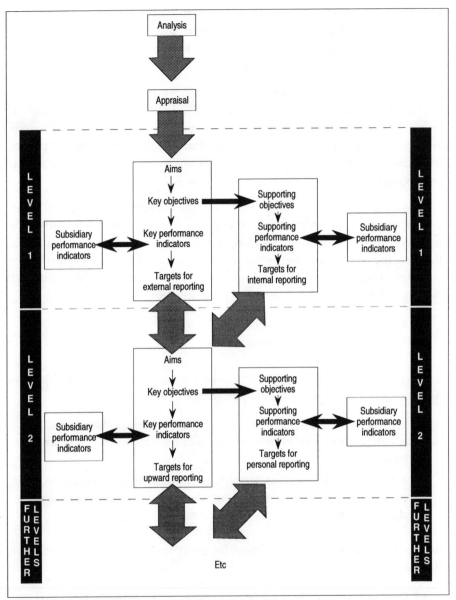

Figure 9.1. The Sunningdale model: aims, objectives and targets.

❏ The aims, objectives and targets cascade

A basic feature of the model is the relationship between aims, objectives, performance indicators and targets. An aim is a broad statement of purpose, often expressed in fairly general terms, which should impart to an organisation, or to part of an organisation, a sense of direction and identity. It should be a reasonably short, clear statement and preferably at least a touch inspiring, something which the staff of the organisation can unite behind. Some people might apply the term *mission statement* to such an expression of purpose.

Objectives move forward from aims, by suggesting specific things which it is intended to achieve in pursuance of the aim. They expand on the aims in a practical way. Then we need to know how we will tell whether we are achieving those objectives or at least moving in the right direction. That brings us to indicators, which are criteria of success. The final stage is the specification of targets. Using the performance indicators as criteria of success, how much success are we striving to achieve by when?

This 'cascade' from aims through objectives and performance indicators to targets can best be illustrated by an example. Consider administering courts. The aim may include a general phrase along the lines of 'a quality service to all those attending the court in a cost-effective manner'. In moving to objectives, it is then necessary to be more specific about what is meant by 'quality service' and 'cost-effective'. This could suggest, amongst other things:

- to reduce delays in bringing cases to court
- to reduce cost per case in real terms.

The next step is to define pretty precisely how progress against these objectives will be assessed. That might lead to performance indicators such as:

- the average number of working days between when the court is notified of the need to hear the case and the date when it is actually heard
- the total number of cases, weighted according to agreed complexity factors, divided by total costs (excluding capital) deflated by the gross domestic product deflator.

The final stage would be to set a target figure for each of these indicators. That might lead us to targets such as:

- to reduce average waiting times to 40 days by 1 January 1996
- to reduce costs per case by 5% in real terms by the end of 1997.

❏ Key and supporting objectives

It will be seen, from Figure 9.1, that reference is made to levels, that means levels within the organisation. Level 1 is the top level within the organisation. In the case of an executive agency, at this level the aims, objectives, indicators and targets would be those applying to the organisation as a whole, those for which the chief executive carries ultimate responsibility. The aims, objectives, indicators and targets at level 2 are then those which apply to the top managers immediately below the level of the chief executive, probably to the individual members of the management team in relation to their own commands. As can be seen from the Figure, the same model illustrated for levels 1 and 2 continues to be replicated through all the remaining levels of the organisation.

One of the principal features replicated at each level is the distinction between key objectives and supporting objectives. This is probably a helpful distinction for both public and private sectors, but, for level 1 at least, it was developed specifically as a result of experience of problems arising in the public sector. Within the private sector accountability to the shareholders may concentrate on financial results, but in the public sector accountability certainly goes more widely than that. However, it is very important to decide on the boundary where the external accountability ends and where managers should start to be free to decide how things are done. The model therefore demands that, when the main objectives are developed during the planning process, a decision is made as to which of those objectives should be reported against outside the organisation, perhaps to the public, perhaps to a minister in a Government department. If the organisation is a Government department, which objectives should be reported to Parliament and to the general public? It will be seen that this distinction is repeated at level 2 and at further levels. The question at these levels is not about external reporting but rather which objectives should be the basis of accountability to one's line manager.

When objectives are agreed during the planning process, they need to be allocated into three groups:

- key objectives for the chief executive or head of the organisation, those objectives against which that person will report performance externally
- supporting objectives for the chief executive or head of the organisation, objectives which need to be achieved if the key objectives are to be met, but decisions on these objectives are an internal matter for the organisation; the chief executive will take personal responsibility within the organisation for achieving these objectives
- key objectives for other managers; again these are objectives which need to be achieved if the key objectives are to be met, again decisions on these objectives are internal to the organisation, but in this case the chief executive delegates responsibility for achieving the objective to another manager, who will be accountable and report achievement to the chief executive.

As an illustration, refer back to the example of court administration. The key objective may be to reduce cost per case. From the planning process it may be decided that the key area where progress has to be made is in reducing staff costs. Reducing staff costs may therefore be a supporting objective for the chief executive. Each manager may then have a key objective to reduce staff costs in their own area of responsibility. Alternatively, if it were decided that effort should be concentrated on reducing the costs associated with the court buildings, that may become a key objective for the support services manager alone.

Another feature of the model is that of subsidiary performance indicators. Within an organisation knowing the outcome against targets is not sufficient in itself, it is also necessary to know why targets have been met or not met. The starting point is the key indicators or the supporting indicators. Managers should then think through what questions they might like to ask about performance on those indicators, and this will lead to the specification of the additional information which the organisation needs to collect and hold. The link between the subsidiary, key and supporting indicators is designed to ensure that the organisation collects what it really needs, not simply what is available, and does not collect what it does not need.

The shaded arrows in Figure 9.1 illustrate that the objectives and targets need to tie together between levels. If the objectives at level 2 are met, it should give assurance that the objectives at level 1 will be met, provided that the chief executive:

a) meets his or her own supporting objectives

b) has chosen the right objectives at level 2.

The model described can also be used to check that objectives fit together horizontally. All the managers at level 2 can check that their objectives are compatible with each other. This is particularly important where delivery objectives and support service objectives are concerned. For example, do the objectives for the information systems manager suggest the provision of the type and quality of services which those delivering services to the public require to enable them to meet their quality objectives?

The comparison of objectives vertically can also help to identify where one level of management does not significantly add value to the efforts of the level below. This shows up where the objectives look very similar at two adjacent levels. There is no problem if one manager has an objective to reduce staff costs, and then five managers at the next level all have objectives to reduce staff costs in their own areas of command. But there could be a problem if only one of those managers has an objective to reduce staff costs, in effect simply duplicating the objective of the manager above.

Finally, is there any difference in the application of the Sunningdale model between strategic plans and business plans? There may be some difference between long-term and medium-term objectives, in particular there is likely to be a heavy emphasis on the core objectives in the strategic plan while the change objectives might feature more strongly in the business plan. The main difference, though, is likely to be that the strategic objectives may not run very far down through the organisation. They may even be restricted entirely to level 1. The medium-term objectives in the business plan are likely to run further down through the organisation, while everyone should have one year objectives in the budget or management plan.

Qualities of good aims, objectives and performance indicators

If aims and objectives are to play a crucial part in ensuring that strategies are delivered, thought needs to be given to the qualities which can equip them for that role. At this point we are not considering whether the right choices have been made, we assume that they have been. Thoughts now turn to how the aims and objectives should be expressed.

❏ Aims

As explained earlier, an aim is a broad statement of purpose and direction. It should be a simple statement, preferably one sentence, which all those working for the organisation can memorise. It should convey a feeling of ultimate purpose, of something worth striving for. The role of an aim is not to give a tight statement of the end result required, but it should convey purpose and values. It provides a constant reference point for all those who work for the organisation and should contribute to delivery of results through uniting people and inspiring them.

As defined here, an aim might also be called a mission statement. There are wide differences of view about the value of mission statements. Some people regard a good mission statement as something which is capable of driving an organisation to success, if you get that right there is little need for anything else. Others find them trite, expressions of motherhood and apple pie, or vague and removed from reality. The view offered here is that a good short aim or mission statement can play a part in inspiring, uniting and motivating people, but that it needs to be backed up by good objectives.

125

Many public sector organisations have aims which are essentially mundane, along the lines of:

> to provide a good service to our customers while achieving continuing improvements in efficiency.

Others prefer something more clearly aspirational:

> to be the best in the world.

The latter has something to commend it, but only if people genuinely feel able to unite behind it. The danger is that senior management might propose such an aim, while most of the staff regard it as pie in the sky, so unrealistic that it earns nothing more than their contempt. An aim which is too far removed in style from the current culture can be counter-productive.

❏ Objectives

What are the signs of an objective which is likely to lead to success in achieving the strategic changes which have been chosen? It is suggested that good objectives should have the following qualities. They should be:

- achievement oriented
- specific
- objective
- ends not means
- few in number
- achievable
- prioritised.

Each of these qualities will now be considered in turn.

Achievement oriented

Objectives relate to the future, they refer to the desired future state. They therefore need to point not just towards doing things, towards activities, but rather towards achievements, towards something which we want to happen or something which we wish to prevent happening. The key to achievement orientation usually lies in the verb, an adjective or adverb. There are numerous examples of objectives which use verbs which describe activities rather than achievement, for example, advise, review, promote, contribute, assist. The key to identifying verbs which describe activities is that it is easy to prove, in an obviously trivial way, that they have been done, for example, 'I have sent a few memos,' or 'I gave some thought to it'. A way to overcome this is often to include an adjective or adverb to describe what would constitute success, for example, to 'advise promptly,' or to 'give advice which meets the needs of ......' As far as possible the words used should have a positive feel to them, to improve, to complete, accurate, timely, to retain, to increase. Even the word 'maintain' can be given a positive feel, as in 'to maintain quality' when other objectives involve reducing costs. The objective 'to support a range of Government activities, notably the promotion of public health and safety, the protection of the environment and defence' seems to be an example where achievement orientation is somewhat lacking.

Specific

Can the desired state of affairs be defined reasonably precisely? This does not mean that everything has to be reduced to simple numerical terms. For example, if an objective is to produce better research reports, can we explain to people what makes a good report? If we ask for improved quality of service, do we mean fewer complaints, goods which do not break down, or higher levels of satisfaction in a customer survey?

Objective

This may sound somewhat tautological, but what it means is that there should be reasonable certainty that, when the actual results emerge, there will be a wide measure of agreement on whether the objective has been achieved or not. This leaves scope for subjective methods of assessment, such as in ice-skating competitions, promotion boards or annual staff reports, but requires that the criteria used in the assessment are clear. The more specific an objective, the higher the probability that it will also be objective.

Ends not means

It might be felt that action planning requires agreement on what must be done, checks that it is done, and rewards when it has been done. Concentrating on the means rather than the ends can, however, lead people to continue following a predetermined course even when circumstances have changed in such a way that that course will no longer lead to the desired result, for example, capital projects continuing to completion even though the need for them has disappeared.

Few

The author has seen examples of individual managers in central Government with as many as forty objectives for the year. Most commentators seem to agree that six to eight objectives for any individual are sufficient, otherwise there is a tendency to lose strategic direction and become too embroiled in matters of detail. The best guide to a reasonable number of objectives is to calculate how much time the manager will effectively be able to devote to each. Start with 260 working days, deduct annual leave and bank holidays, deduct the time required for general managerial duties such as management boards, deduct time spent in training or at conferences, then divide the number of days left by the number of objectives. Does the result suggest that the manager is able to add real value?

Achievable

Objectives should not simply be imposed. If they are to be effective, they almost certainly need to be agreed. They should emerge from a participative planning process, with a proper balance of top-down and bottom-up. Achievability has two aspects:

- the objective should not be hopelessly ambitious, such as reducing unit costs by a large percentage in an impossibly short time
- the organisation or the individual should have the formal powers to achieve the objective.

It is the second of these which frequently creates problems in the public sector. There are many cases where public servants have to achieve results indirectly, (eg through local authorities, or non-departmental public bodies, or by influencing behaviour.) This can easily be used as an excuse for ending up with no objectives at all! In the private sector, most managers will depend in part on external events, but good performance involves showing an ability to respond to those events and cope with them. It is suggested that, where there is a doubt about whether an objective lies within a person's power to deliver it, the test should be whether someone else can be found to take responsibility for the objective instead. If there is no one else, either the first person should accept it or a reorganisation is needed to improve the clarity of responsibilities.

Prioritised

Finally, it is important that objectives should be prioritised. In practice, external circumstances are always likely to change during a year, and this may mean that it is not possible to achieve all objectives simultaneously or that it is possible to achieve more than was originally expected. If there is a clear sense of priorities, individual managers will be able to respond to such circumstances without going back to rework the whole business plan.

❏ Qualities of good performance indicators

A good deal of emphasis has been placed on the need for objectives which make it clear what is expected. This clarity will be reinforced by good performance indicators, which define how success will actually be assessed. So what are the qualities of good performance indicators? The checklist offered is that indicators should be:

- relevant
- unambiguous
- cheatproof
- low cost
- capable of comparison with others
- simple
- useful.

Relevant

The concept of relevance, in the present context, can be divided into four elements:

- related to objectives
- at the right level of responsibility for the manager concerned
- driven by factors felt to be appropriate
- of statistical significance.

If the Sunningdale model illustrated in Figure 9.1 is followed, there should be no problem with the first two of these points. The model shows clearly that performance indicators follow from objectives, and the indicators will therefore be suited to the level of responsibility if the objective is.

As far as the third point is concerned, the question to ask is, over the period under consideration what factors are most likely to be the major influence on the level of this indicator and are these factors the ones in which we are interested? For example, in comparing cost per pupil between schools, the major influence is likely to be school size, not managerial efficiency. But in looking at cost per pupil, is it actually being recognised for what it is, simply an indicator of school size? To examine managerial efficiency we must restrict the comparison to schools of similar size.

The point about statistical significance is very important when it comes to setting target values. The key factor in statistical significance is the absolute size of the sample. There is little use in setting a target of improving from 85% to 86%, if the sample survey can only give us the answers accurate to within three percentage points.

Unambiguous

The need for indicators to be unambiguous emphasises again the relationship between indicators and objectives. The most important issue is, do we know whether we want the value of the indicator to go up or down? For example, an increase in drugs seizures could be a sign that Customs Officers have improved their effectiveness. Alternatively, it could be a sign that more drugs are entering the country, and easier to find.

There can also be problems of ambiguity when people come to describe what particular indicators mean, especially if those indicators are in the form of ratios. For example, there are cases where death rates have been mixed up with survival rates, cases where an increase from 40% to 44% has been interpreted as a 4% improvement instead of a 10% improvement, and confusion about whether raising a number from 100 to 300 represents a twofold or threefold increase. If indicators are to serve their purpose in strategic management, they must be capable of unambiguous interpretation in lay terms; they must not be the preserve of the numerate specialist, they must help to give direction and purpose to every manager.

Cheatproof

Performance indicators give more precision to objectives. It is therefore important that they encourage desired behaviour. The literature is full of examples of indicators which have encouraged perverse behaviour, such as lorry drivers driving their vehicles around empty in order to clock up miles, of academics creating circles to refer to each other's work to increase the number of citations, or people passing papers to each other for 'comment' to reduce the time the papers spend on their own desks. And what about creative accounting to increase apparent profits in the commercial world? The test is to ask oneself, what would I do if I were being judged by my performance against this indicator? If there is a danger that a single indicator against a particular objective would be misleading, it may be worth considering a second indicator alongside the first to guard against distortion.

Low cost

Information is essential to any business or operation, but information gathering is not the primary business, unless you happen to be the Central Statistical Office. The secret to containing the cost of producing performance indicators is to ensure that the indicators represent information which is required for day-to-day management and which is collected fairly automatically in the course of undertaking business.

Information can often be collected nowadays as a by-product of the use of information technology for many routine processes. For example, if computers are used in casework it becomes very easy to record when the case was opened, the category of the case, the types of action taken, and the time when the case was closed.

Capable of comparison with others

Standards of performance and levels of efficiency tend mostly to be relative concepts rather than absolutes. A figure means little in itself, but takes on more significance when compared with:

- performance of similar operations elsewhere in the organisation
- performance of similar operations in other organisations
- performance in a previous period of time
- an agreed standard of performance, such as a Charter standard.

The potential value of the first two categories in the planning process was discussed under the heading of benchmarking in Chapter 6.

Simple

The intention is that the indicators should influence people's behaviour. It is therefore vital that people should know:

- what the indicator means
- how they can influence it.

The need for simplicity can be a problem with indicators at the top of the organisation. The objectives and indicators at that level may need to bring together a number of elements of performance into a single objective and a single indicator. For example, if an organisation, such as a court, has to deal with a number of types of cases, it has to find a way of weighting these cases together to obtain an overall indicator of workload. It is important to do this, otherwise top managers end up looking at details, at each type of case, rather than concentrating on the corporate issues, and this can leave a major vacuum, a lack of strategic direction. The danger, though, is that if people do not understand the aggregate indicator it will not be used to help manage the business, it will be produced only because it has to be.

Useful

It will always be difficult (impossible?) to find an indicator which satisfies all the criteria set out above. However, the primary requirement is not that the indicators are perfect, but that they are useful to managers, in clarifying what has to be achieved, in providing information which identifies the need for action, and in posing questions which managers ultimately find helpful.

Project management

The emphasis, in ensuring action, has been placed on the use of clear objectives, performance indicators and targets, and on making clear who is responsible for achieving what. In some cases it will emerge that major change programmes are necessary, and that it will be some considerable time before the final outputs can be examined and compared with what is desired. This could be a major capital project such as new buildings or a major refurbishment, it could be the relocation of a major group of staff, it could be development of a new service, an organisational change, or a cultural change. In this case the manager's performance will tend to be monitored by reference to project milestones through the life of the project, until the final outcome can be evaluated.

The manager in this situation will need to employ the normal project management techniques to help to ensure that the project is well directed and that desired outcomes are achieved. This subject is another of those which has formed the basis of books in its own right. Suffice it to say here that attention would have to be given to issues such as:

- clarity of project objectives and the project definition
- choosing the right project teams, with the right balance of skills and of personal attributes
- planning the project, identifying the necessary sequence of steps and how they fit together, how they depend upon each other
- consulting interested parties and communicating progress to them
- securing the necessary resources, physical and financial, including the co-operation of all parties who can influence success
- information systems, to permit the monitoring of progress, physical and financial
- proper change control procedures.

Project management contains a lot of common sense, but there are techniques which can help which need to be learned. Those entrusted with projects for the first time should certainly undertake some training or study to acquaint them with the wide body of knowledge on the subject.

At the top of the organisation, it may well be found, indeed it seems to be found increasingly, that the issues identified require projects which cut across the standard hierarchical boundaries. In this case the chief executive and management team will need to devote some effort to ensuring that the organisation has arrangements to support such projects, for example:

- identifying project managers and creating cross-command project teams
- project reporting, which does not follow the normal command lines.

The commitment of top management to these projects will be critical.

As a final point, it is worth bearing in mind that every manager with an output or outcome to deliver needs to have his or her own action plans, or private project plan, to ensure delivery. What actions will be taken, in what order, when, with whom? Therefore, in a sense, every manager needs some acquaintance with the general principles of project planning. The bigger and the more complex the project, the more formal and knowledgeable that acquaintance needs to be.

Total quality management

It is unusual nowadays to find any organisation, whether in the public or private sector, where quality is not an issue to emerge in the strategic management processes. Responsibility for action on quality could be left to individual managers, with the requirement for continuing improvements in quality embraced in their objectives and targets. However, many have found that achieving continuing improvements in quality across the organisation requires a concerted approach, which ensures that everyone from top to bottom of the organisation is:

- aware of quality
- committed to quality
- active in improving quality.

In total quality management, quality is not seen as implying high cost. In many respects the opposite is the case. Building quality procedures into design, into handling of materials, into training, will help to reduce costs. At the most basic level getting things right first time avoids all the costs associated with putting them right later, whether through scrapping rejects, replacing or repairing defective goods, or through compensating consumers.

There are a number of key elements in applying the concepts of total quality management to make things happen. The first is commitment, and visible commitment, from the top of the organisation. The commitment of a chief executive is vital, but then there needs to be a high level steering group, perhaps known as a quality council, to co-ordinate and manage the programme of quality improvement. The committee also needs a leading light, who will undertake prime responsibility for what is, in effect, the project management.

A second feature of total quality management is team working. Individual projects are selected, processes or issues for improvement, which will be tackled by process improvement teams or quality teams, who will be given clear objectives regarding the benefits required from their efforts. Many of these teams will need to work across the normal functional boundaries.

A third feature of total quality management is the emphasis on measuring quality. The name of W Edwards Deming is closely associated with the development of total quality management, and his background was in statistics. Measurement of quality does not necessarily mean hard numerical measures, it can involve measures, or indicators, of behaviour and attitudes. There is, however, an emphasis on examining the evidence of improvement, on providing data to back up claims of improvement.

Creating sustained improvement in performance is not easy. Approaches such as 'total quality management' can be treated as panaceas, the obvious answer, and enthusiastically adopted, but without thought as to the demanding conditions for success. Some of these conditions might be thought to be common sense, such as allocating sufficient resources to the teams, giving sufficient management time, but too often the rush of enthusiasm means that people do not take time to think these things through. There are also questions of choosing the right types of people, good leaders, teams with a good blend of personalities and of preferred methods of working. There are also some particular techniques which staff throughout the organisation may need to learn, particularly those associated with scientific methods, the collection, analysis and understanding of data. Managers are advised to seek expert advice to help them in the early stages of any total quality programme.

Business process reengineering

Another popular approach to achieving desired change at the present time is business process reengineering (BPR). At one extreme the term is used to cover what might be called 'process improvement,' relying quite heavily on traditional tools from the organisation and methods kit. In this guise, individual processes can be mapped, particular elements questioned, and shorter routes sought. At the other extreme, BPR may be used as an approach to strategic planning, rethinking the whole purpose of the business. BPR is offered here as a tool to help in action planning, to ensure results in an area where a need for major improvement has been identified during the planning cycle. It is one way of tackling an issue. To see where it is most likely to be appropriate, it might be helpful to identify its key features.

First, BPR concerns processes. These are likely to run across functional boundaries, across the normal hierarchy. They are processes which are meaningful from a customer's point of view, which should add value to the service offered, but within the normal hierarchy no one takes responsibility for the whole process. The most obvious example of this is where a customer has to go from one person to another to someone else and then perhaps back to the first again to get what one wants.

The second key point is that BPR involves reengineering, not improvement. It requires radical rethinking of how things are done. The intention is not to reduce costs by 10% but rather to slash them by 75%, not to reduce delivery times from 40 days to 35, but rather to cut them to two days. In the experience of BPR, there is a (public sector) example where a service which at one time took over seven weeks to deliver from beginning to end was reengineered to be completed in a single day. In the words of Hammer and Champy (1993) reengineering is:

> the fundamental rethinking and radical redesign of business processes to achieve dramatic improvements in critical, contemporary measures of performance such as cost, quality, service and speed.

It involves radical rethinking, questioning whether particular elements of the process need to be done at all.

Reengineering originated in the private sector, in recognition of the imperative of meeting global competition. Looking at the strength of the competition, it was clear that continuous improvements in quality and efficiency would never be capable of matching the competition; step change was necessary, totally different ways of doing things. While in most parts of the public sector there is not the same competitive imperative, the pressures on public expenditure are such as to make the potential of BPR an attractive proposition. BPR is explicitly mentioned in the recent White Paper (Cm 2627, 1994) *Continuity and Change*, as a valuable tool for improving efficiency.

Many of the points made about project management generally apply equally to BPR. A reengineering exercise is very much a project, and a project to introduce major change. Key success factors are likely to be:

- a champion at very senior level
- a dedicated team, working full time on the exercise
- good benchmarking, and the setting of some really visionary (stretching) targets for improvement
- good process mapping, to provide a clear understanding of what is done
- clear understanding of the process as seen from the customer's angle
- creative thinking
- good communications, to give a clear understanding among the workforce of why change is necessary, recognising their values and attitudes
- a high profile for the exercise, ensuring that it is not just one of many exercises proceeding together
- good implementation plan
- stamina.

Looking at examples of successful reengineering projects, a regular feature is that they cut out some conventional hierarchical barriers. They tend to move towards a one-stop shop, whereby one person takes full responsibility for an individual case, instead of papers having to pass progressively through many pairs of hands. The process mapping often reveals that a large proportion of the time taken to complete a case involves the papers sitting in the internal post or in in-trays, while the time actually taken working on the case is quite short.

Business process reengineering is a helpful approach, having identified an issue which cries out for radical improvement, to establishing a practical solution and implementing it. Success, though, will only come if there is strong commitment, adequate resources, and a willingness to keep going when the extent of the possible changes and of the potential opposition looks daunting.

References

Cm 2627 (1994) *The Civil Service: Continuity and Change* London HMSO

Hammer, M. and Champy, J. (1993) *Reengineering the Corporation: A Manifesto for Business Revolution*, London Nicholas Brealey Publishing

Chapter 10

Documentation and communication

The quotation from a note produced by the Treasury at the end of Chapter 1 emphasised that it is the planning process which is of greatest importance, not the written plans which are produced at the end. Nevertheless a great deal of emphasis has been placed on the production of written plans within the public sector, particularly as a key element in the relationship between sponsored bodies and their sponsoring Government department. The framework documents of executive agencies all require the preparation of plans and their submission to the appropriate parent department. The danger is that the writing of such a plan can come to be seen as a bureaucratic exercise, required by an outside party. The planning process then loses validity as a tool for helping to manage the agency effectively. For these reasons, our consideration of documentation is placed firmly in the context of the third stage of strategic management, the action stage. Documentation should be used as an aid to ensuring action, to communicating what is expected.

So what documentation is required? We consider this in three stages:

- the audience: who needs to be informed and the nature of their interest
- questions of appropriate content
- alternative methods of communication to the written word.

The audience

Before deciding what documentation to produce, it is necessary to think of all the groups of people who are potentially interested and to identify in general terms what they would like to know and what it is appropriate to tell them. (There could be good reasons for treating some information as commercial in confidence, and the plans of some public sector bodies may need to omit some material which is subject to security classification.) This exercise may well, in fact usually will, suggest that more than one version of the plan needs to be written.

❏ Interested parties

The groups potentially interested in seeing a written plan will vary from organisation to organisation, but the following groups are usually strong candidates:

- a sponsoring or parent Government department, both ministers and officials
- Parliament
- staff of the organisation, senior management, middle management and the more junior staff
- customers, those for whom the service is provided, and perhaps the general public
- lobby groups with a particular interest in the organisation's activities
- suppliers and partners
- the media.

Some public sector organisations will be bound by statute or, in the case of an executive agency, by a framework document, to make a written plan available to specified parties or to the public as a whole.

❏ Their interest

In the private sector the planning process will require strategic business units to submit proposals to the company headquarters for consideration. These proposals, almost certainly prepared in accordance with guidelines issued from the centre, will be reviewed by headquarters alongside proposals from other strategic business units, and there will probably be a meeting to go through the proposals. Agreement will be reached on the resources available to the business unit, on the targets, financial and non-financial, which it is required to meet, allowing the business unit's plan to be finalised, as the basis of subsequent action and monitoring. In effect, the original proposal is a bidding document.

Such bidding documents will play an equally important part in the strategic management processes in the public sector. These documents may come from individual directorates to the top of a department, from individual commands to a chief executive or from an executive agency or non-departmental public body to the department which funds it. What will the recipient be looking for? Firstly:

- information to add to other information to allow the implications of all the plans received to be put together to give an aggregate picture for the organisation as a whole

- information to permit judgement on the strength of the case for the resources proposed.

The document will therefore need to contain:

- some pre-specified data, to add to data from others
- justification for the proposals, an explanation of the thinking which led to the proposals.

However, there should be no need for details of the plans of individual groups within the organisation, as the sponsoring body should be concentrating on the overall picture, leaving issues at the lower level for the organisation to decide for itself.

Turning now to senior managers within the organisation, they will wish to know about the actions, objectives and targets for their individual commands. At the bidding document stage their interest will be a general one. However, for managing the organisation, they will need to know their own targets once the targets for the top of the organisation have been set and once the resources available to the organisation have been *agreed*. Will they wish to see all of the justification for the proposals and the final choices? They may, for the record, but if involved in those decisions in the first place may feel that they can remember the reasoning, and the prime concern now is what has to be delivered.

Moving down to the middle managers and more junior staff, they may wish to be informed of the overall strategy, of the decisions made at the top of the organisation, but may be they will not feel the need for much detail. They will wish to have a record, however, of what it now implies for them, their own objectives, targets and resources.

The interest of customers may be limited to the implications for the level of service to be offered and how much it is going to cost them. Whether they have a broader interest in the general direction of the organisation will depend upon the nature of this organisation itself. The focus of lobbies is likely to be fairly narrow as well, concentrating on the cause which they espouse. Suppliers and partners will concentrate on the levels of activities which affect them directly.

Finally, what would be the interest of Parliament or of the general public? The former at least will wish to know about the overall policy and the direction of change, but it is unclear how far they would wish to see the justification for the proposals.

In the light of this discussion, how many different sets of documentation might be necessary? To avoid undue effort, it is desirable to consolidate as many of the interests as possible into a single document, but it might still be necessary, depending upon the nature of the organisation, to produce a number of documents. The following might be candidates from which to choose:

- a fully argued document, covering basically the top level corporate issues, the proposed strategies, policies, objectives, targets and resources, with justification for the decisions proposed
- a supplement for senior staff internally showing the key points for individual commands
- for each member of staff, a document setting out their specific personal objectives
- a version of the first document above with much of the argumentation and any sensitive commercial-in-confidence information removed
- a short glossy summarising key points.

Some questions on content

The issue of how much argumentation and justification to include has been covered above. There is no right answer, it is simply a question which needs to be addressed by top management in the circumstances of any particular case.

❏ Openness

A related question is that of openness, particularly openness about problems, about weaknesses and threats. In a published document it is unlikely that one would wish to say much about specific competitive threats and the strategies to deal with them; that could simply provoke pre-emptive strikes from the competitors. On the other hand, even in a public document one might wish to draw attention to potential difficulties, in order to manage public expectations about future performance.

In documentation for one's own staff, one has to be open about weaknesses and threats if one wishes to use the plan to encourage the staff to action which will overcome the problems. In submitting proposals to a sponsoring department, the decision on what to include may well reflect the quality of relationships generally.

A number of problems arose in the 1970s when nationalised industries failed to warn their departments and the Treasury about problems in advance. The result was that, when the problem materialised, Government was forced to agree additional funding, because it was too late to undertake corrective action. In one sense this was very effective in securing additional funding; it reflected a poor relationship between industries, departments and the Treasury, in particular a feeling in the industries that, if they warned about the problems, they would not receive a balanced hearing. On the other hand, the experience merely served to cause relationships to deteriorate further, 'confirming' the impression that the industries were poorly managed. It is recommended that, when submitting proposals to the 'funding' body, whether a Government department or a more senior level in one's own organisation, it is best to be open about the issues. If there is some inherent reluctance to do this, ask why. It will probably be because of a lack of trust somewhere, so concentrate on trying to put that right.

❑ Leaving options open

Another question to consider is, should some options be left open? Documents submitted at the bidding stage should contain options. Those looking at these 'draft plans' will wish to consider the benefits of additional funding or the consequences of less funding than the guideline figures on which the central case has been based. It is really quite inappropriate for plans to be finalised, as many plans of non-departmental public bodies have tended to be in the past, prior to decisions on resource allocations. When submitting proposals to be taken into account in the public expenditure survey, it is important to include a balanced account of the implications of different levels of funding, then the plan can be finalised when the resource allocation has been agreed. Only at that stage can the plan really be the basis of managing and monitoring the business.

❑ Hidden agendas

Questions are sometimes raised about 'hidden agendas' in plans. There is no doubt that, on occasions, issues identified in the planning cycles will be of such significance that there will be some reluctance to announce decisions about them. For example, it may become evident that a major part of the operation will need to be closed down in about 18 months' time. Announcing that now will have an immediate impact on current performance and cause further damage to the organisation's future prospects. The advice, though, is to avoid hidden agendas and to be open, with the organisation's own staff at least. If people learn that a particular strategic or business plan failed to reveal something important, it will be very difficult to win their co-operation and gain their confidence in the planning processes in future. The best approach is probably, having identified the need for unpleasant action, to announce the fact and take action quickly.

❑ Suggestions on content

So, can any guidance be given on the content of the various documents? A 'draft plan', a document submitted to a funding body to contribute to decisions on resource allocation, almost certainly needs to make a case for, to justify, what is proposed. The starting point should probably be a report of the planning process itself. In the case of a strategic plan that might suggest the contents listed in Figure 10.1, for a business plan the contents might be as in Figure 10.2. This may look rather a lot but there is no need for each heading to constitute a whole chapter on its own. The extent of the argumentation and justification will depend upon the importance of particular proposals and on how finely balanced the options are. A second point is that the document should concentrate on the issues and choices at the corporate level and should not normally go into detail about the proposals for individual commands. There are many examples at the moment where written plans include a great deal of information about parts of an organisation or individual programmes, detail which implicitly invites the sponsoring body to question matters which should lie within the powers of the organisation itself to determine.

Once funding levels and any modifications to the proposals have been agreed, a revised document will have to be produced. If the changes are minimal it may be necessary to do no more than produce an addendum to record the changes. However, the revised version will be for a different audience, and consideration might be given to removing much of the argumentation and concentrating on the conclusions. Then further versions might be produced for other audiences, perhaps summaries of conclusions most relevant to the particular audience.

Draft strategic plan

1. Reasons for producing a new strategic plan.
2. Review of performance against past strategic and business plans.
3. Summary of mandates.
4. Summary of stakeholder anaylsis.
5. Summary of external analysis and key assumptions.
6. Summary of internal analysis.
7. Strategic issues identified.
8. Options examined.
9. Summary of appraisals
10. Suggested aim and vision of the future.
11. Proposed key initiatives and projects.
12. Suggested long term key objectives, performance indicators and targets.
13. Resource requirements for preferred option.
14. Priorities, and implications of the other main options for aims, key objectives, targets and resource requirements.
15. Summary of key data for preferred and main options.

Figure 10.1. Possible contents of a strategic plan submitted for approval.

Draft business plan

1. Summary of strategy.
2. Review of recent performance and external developments.
3. Key assumptions.
4. Issues identified.
5. Options examined.
6. Summary of appraisals.
7. Preferred options within baseline figures issued by parent body at beginning of the planning process.
8. Proposed key objectives within baseline and associated performance indicators.
9. Summary of initiatives to be pursued to achieve proposed key objectives.
10. Proposed key targets, including financial implications, within baseline.
11. Priorities for additional funding, preferred funding level and the implications of these and of any reductions in funding on key objectives, indicators, targets and initiatives.
12. Compilation of information specified in any guidelines issued by parent body at beginning of the planning process.

Figure 10.2. Possible contents of a business plan submitted for approval.

Within the organisation further more detailed documentation will be required to explain what is expected of particular commands or particular individuals. Indeed, each command might have its own plan, and each individual will certainly need his or her own forward job plan and personal objectives compatible with the higher level plans. At a minimum these plans for separate commands and particular individuals might consist of no more than objectives, targets and resources, but it may be decided to include some description of the thinking processes as well. Helping any staff concerned to see the reasoning may serve both to increase their commitment and their understanding of what is required from them.

Alternatives to the written word

The problem with communicating by the written word is that some people will not bother to read what is sent to them. Written documentation seems likely to remain the primary form of communication, however, where:

- arguments have to be carefully studied, such as in the case of a draft plan submitted for approval
- factual items which will need to be referred to regularly, as would be the case with objectives and targets.

Other forms of communication might be considered where at a particular point one wishes:

- to explain the corporate objectives to all of the staff
- to explain the thinking behind the strategies and objectives
- to inform outside interests about the plans.

Inside the organisation, an alternative to written documentation is the use of cascade briefing, that is briefing through the normal lines of command. So, for example, each member of the management board might brief their own senior staff who would then brief their staff. This approach has the benefit of face-to-face communication, whereas communication through the written word can appear cold and distant. However, there are two essential conditions which must be satisfied for it to be successful:

- it must be well organised
- it must be possible to rely on the commitment of the line managers to the strategy.

Good organisation means in particular that it must be done quickly and at the same speed throughout the organisation. Resentment will build up very quickly if some groups feel that others are being told important things well before they are. The second point concerns the message actually given. Is it possible to be certain that the same message will be given, or will the managers present views of their own? Remember, though, that even when the same words are spoken or written to different people, it does not mean that they hear the same message. The face-to-face communication of cascade briefing, the style in which the message is delivered, can, if done well, do more to ensure that the same message is received than can written documentation.

An alternative to cascade briefing is to organise a series of meetings addressed by the chief executive. This should be more likely to deliver the same (or very similar) words in the same (or very similar) styles to everyone. The feasibility of this will depend upon the nature of the organisation, particularly upon how dispersed it is. In some cases organisations have produced videos where they are very dispersed. A video ensures that exactly the same words are conveyed in exactly the same style to everyone. However, this still does not guarantee that the same message is received, and there is no opportunity for interaction, questions and answer, to clarify the situation. Videos can also be counterproductive if those appearing in them are not relaxed in front of a camera!

Chapter 11

Some general issues

In this chapter we try to address some of the most frequent general questions which are put to lecturers at the Civil Service College during courses on strategic management. The issues considered are:

- what are the essential differences between planning in the public and private sectors
- how should the top-down and bottom-up elements of planning be linked together
- how can we cope with the level of uncertainty; does this uncertainty mean that planning is a waste of time
- where does the currently very popular concept of strategic control fit into all this
- should we use outside help in the strategic management processes?

Public and private sectors

One of the difficulties in trying to establish differences between strategic management in the public and private sectors is that of distinguishing inherent differences, differences of principle, from differences of practice. There may then be a further distinction between differences of practice which seem justified and differences of practice which imply that the public sector is not doing things well.

❏ Freedom to choose

One point which is often made is that, in the public sector, there is little choice as to what an organisation should do. There is certainly a great deal of truth in this. Legislation has to be enacted, the civil servants have to implement the Government's policies, executive agencies have to do what is stipulated in their framework documents. This is why the strategic planning element of strategic management includes the review of mandates. The danger, though, as explained in Chapter 4, is that public sector organisations will tend to assume that they are more constrained than they are. Ultimately, however, major changes in service may still require authority, through the planning cycle, from Government ministers.

In comparing this situation with the private sector, it is easy to exaggerate the difference. Textbooks on strategic management for the private sector seem to be aimed primarily at the management of large corporations, which certainly do have a good deal of freedom to change their business. Strategic business units within these corporations will be more constrained, they will have to work within the strategies of the corporation as a whole. Within the public sector most corporate planning, most strategic management, is currently undertaken at the level of executive agencies or non-departmental public bodies, which are accountable, though in varying ways, to Government departments. In other words, most of the planning is done at the equivalent of strategic business unit level, rather than at corporate level. If planning were done at that corporate level, there might be a degree of freedom of choice more akin to that available to a private corporation. In practice, strategic management processes are not applied to the development of policy at the top of Government departments, but there is no reason why they should not be. Virtually all of the techniques of analysis and appraisal described in this book can be used to develop policy.

❏ Complexity of the planning cycle

One of the frustrations for those involved in planning at the level of executive agencies, non-departmental public bodies, or groups within Government departments is the timescale. Planning seems not only continuous, which it should be, but endless, which conveys a different feeling. Draft plans, proposals, have to be submitted to the top of Government departments about April, to allow the department to assess the plans and construct its own proposals to forward to the Treasury in May. It is November before funding levels for departments are announced, and it then takes a little longer for departments to review the outcome before informing their agencies, sponsored bodies and internal groups of their final targets and resources.

This elongated cycle is undoubtedly inherent in the nature of the public sector. The public sector as a whole amounts to about 45% of the United Kingdom's national income, which means that it is somewhat larger than any individual private corporation. Relationships are inevitably more complex. Many of those required to prepare plans are, in effect, at the third level of management or lower within the public sector as a whole. The true comparison for such bodies should be with groups within strategic business units within corporations.

Having said all that, the delay between Government departments submitting proposals in May and being notified of the outcome in November is a good deal longer than any strategic business unit would expect. This delay reflects in part the large number of departments and in part the complexity of the issues, given the political dimensions to them. It is currently something with which public servants will have to live.

❏ Complexity of the objectives

It is undoubtedly an over-simplification to suggest that private sector companies have one very simple objective, namely to make a profit, though that thought is often advanced by managers in the public sector. Back in the 1950s books were being written to suggest that, in large corporations, the objectives being pursued by managers were somewhat more complex than profit maximisation. In recent times there has been a good deal of interest in non-financial objectives, such as market share, internal culture and external perceptions, which are regarded as vital to long-term survival. Pursuing narrow financial objectives on their own could in fact damage prospects for long-term survival.

The private sector has also tended, in recent years, to recognise the concept of stakeholders. There are many groupings which can, directly or indirectly, affect a company's success. The most obvious example is probably environmental interests, which have led many companies to establish 'green' policies.

Having said all that, it probably remains true that the stakeholder analysis for most public sector bodies is going to be more complex than the stakeholder analysis for most private sector companies. As a result the key objectives will be more difficult to determine. It will be more difficult to establish clarity of vision and of direction. The inference of this, though, seems to the writer to be that the planning processes take on more importance in the public sector. People still need a sense of direction, the imperative to provide good services is still there, but we will have to put more effort into determining what that direction should be and how good service can be defined.

❏ Accountability

A whole chapter has been devoted to documentation and communication, a subject which features rarely, if at all, in books on strategic management written with a primarily private sector audience in mind. Issues of internal communication will apply equally to both sectors. Issues of communication between a body and its parent or sponsoring organisation are also likely to be similar. If there is a difference, it might arise because those receiving proposals from a strategic business unit are more familiar with the circumstances, activities and performance of that unit than many of those in Government departments who receive proposals from agencies and sponsored bodies. The more familiar the recipient is with the business, the less the need for argumentation and justification of proposals in a written submission. The idea of a Fraser figure, someone in a Government department who acts as the key point of contact with and who becomes familiar with a particular executive agency, may reduce the need for written documentation.

When it comes to communication with external interests, the public sector is in a different position from the private sector. Many public sector organisations are formally required to publish their plans. This can place all sorts of pressures on an organisation. Examples are:

- to express objectives and targets in as vague a way as possible; given that the environment is uncertain, one does not wish to be held tightly to account for targets which are known to be risky

- to be vague about certain strategies where publication might itself lead others to take action to hinder achievement of the objectives

- to keep some agendas hidden, where premature disclosure may exacerbate the problems.

The important thing is that these pressures on the 'public plan' should not be allowed to prevent the planning process from tackling the issues properly. Recognising that the public plan might be a different document from that submitted to a funding organisation and different from the working document used internally is important in this respect. This means that commentators should be wary of looking at published plans and criticising them for not being something which they were never intended to be.

Some plans have, in the past, been criticised for looking like bidding documents rather than plans. In most cases they were in fact intended to be bidding documents; the published document was the one submitted to a funding body as a contribution to that body's resource allocation process. There is a real question mark as to whether the published plan should be that document or one produced when the resource allocations and targets have been agreed. Other published plans have been criticised as not providing an adequate basis for managing the business internally, when there was separate unpublished documentation for that purpose. Deciding what to publish is no easy matter. While there are genuine reasons for not wishing to publish every detail, it is important to recognise that accountability to Parliament and to the public is a proper demand on public sector organisations.

Top-down and bottom-up planning

The notion of top-down and bottom-up planning was introduced in Chapter 1 in the section on participation. At this point, the emphasis is more on the practicalities of bringing together any top-down vision with bottom-up practical ideas to create the right overall blend, a practical, visionary plan perhaps.

The strategic management process described in this text has three stages:

- analysis
- appraisal
- action.

The analysis stage leads up to a set of issues, which are then carried forward to the appraisal stage. There can be some issues at the corporate level, some at the level of individual commands below that. In practical terms, it is suggested that the process could proceed in the stages shown in Figure 11.1. There will inevitably be variations in individual cases in the light of particular circumstances, but the process shown may serve as a starting point.

One point to note is that the heads of individual commands may also be members of the management team. Only in large organisations are management teams not likely to have direct accountability for particular areas of activity. Secondly, the responsibilities shown in the left-hand column of Figure 11.1 at each stage represent ultimate responsibilities, but a variety of people may, and should, be involved in the work leading up to the final decision points. Thirdly, only one iteration is shown between the initial proposals from the commands and teams and final agreement; in practice more iterations may be needed, while sometimes no iteration at all may be necessary. Fourthly, the process illustrated covers two levels within the organisation. It may be desirable to incorporate a third level as well; in effect the heads of commands would issue guidelines to the next level of management, says heads of units, and would then review proposals from the heads of units before preparing their own proposals to put to the chief executive. Ideally, it might be argued, this process should incorporate every level of management, but in practice the timescales required for the various iterations would make this impractical. Therefore, it is probably necessary to cut the process off at some level, and then take the decisions made at that level as mandates within which levels below have to work. This is likely to be more acceptable if the people below the cut-off level contributed to the higher level decisions.

Stage 1 Chief executive and management team	1. Identify corporate issues. 2. Agree which issues need to be resolved immediately at corporate level. 3. Appraise options for these issues and resolve them. 4. Delegate resolution of remaining issues to individual commands within the hierarchy or to cross-command project teams. 5. Incorporate all of the above into planning guidelines, including indicative targets, and issue to the heads of command and project team leaders.
Stage 2 Individual commands and project teams	1. Individual commands identify further issues unique to their own areas. 2. Commands prepare proposals to resolve all issues, those remitted to them and those which they have identified. 3. Project teams prepare proposals to resolve issues remitted to them. 4. Commands and teams submit proposals to chief executive.
Stage 3 Chief executive and planning team	1. Planning team consolidate and review proposals, compare the outcome with the planning guidelines, and report conclusions to chief exective. 2. Chief executive holds bilateral meetings with heads of command and project teams and requests modifications to proposals where necessary.
Stage 4 Individual commands and project teams	1. Commands and teams present revised proposals and submit them to planning team.
Stage 5 Chief executive and management team	1. Revised proposals are consolidated by planning team and compared with planning guidelines. 2. Consolidated picture is reviewed by management team and agreement reached.

Figure 11.1. Merging the top-down and bottom-up.

Coping with uncertainty

In the early days of formal planning processes, it may have been felt that planning would help to reduce uncertainty. There are still people who implicitly hold this view, for example when they say that they cannot plan because they are demand led. It is true that they cannot plan the level of demand, but they can still plan how best to organise their operations to cope effectively with sudden changes in the level of demand. The emphasis nowadays in strategic management is not on reducing uncertainty, rather it is on coping with uncertainty. So, what are the principles for building a flexible organisation which can cope with uncertainty?

❏ Delegation and empowerment

To cope effectively with rapid changes, organisations have to be capable of taking decisions quickly. Problems will often be spotted first by those people who work at the service delivery end. How long will it take for those problems to come to the attention of those who have the authority to make a decision about the response? The longer the links in the chain between those who spot the problem and those who can take decisions, the longer it will take to make decisions and to transmit those decisions back to those who need to act differently. All the time information is passing up through the management chain and back down again, the problem could be growing and performance could be deteriorating. Hence organisations are better placed to cope with uncertainty if:

- they have flat structures
- those near the front line have authority to take decisions.

Reducing the number of links in the chain of command is not just a way of reducing overheads and increasing job satisfaction, it can also help to maintain effective performance in the face of major changes in the environment.

❏ Understanding the environment and the objectives

Before a decision can be made to respond to a change of circumstances, that change of circumstances has to be spotted. This means that the managers concerned have to:

- understand the external environment
- know what matters
- monitor and watch what matters
- know what sort of decision is required.

These conditions are more likely to be met if managers participate in the planning process, particularly if they join in at the external analysis stage. This makes them think about the environment, look at factual information about it and identify the assumptions which are critical to the business. Involving managers in building scenarios, for example, will not only probably improve the scenarios, it will also help to build the managers' awareness. If they know which assumptions are most important, they will also know what to watch out for. Their understanding of critical factors will be enhanced if they are aware of the results of sensitivity tests, and their ability to take good decisions will be enhanced if they understand and share a commitment to the organisation's key objective.

Encouraging participation in the strategic management processes is thus not simply a matter of increasing staff commitment and contributing greater knowledge to the decisions, it should also help to create an organisation which is more able to cope with unexpected changes.

❏ Concentrate on ends not means

The nature of objectives can also be important in enabling managers to respond to uncertainty. If their objectives concentrate on means rather than ends they are effectively constrained to keep acting in a specified way however the world changes. If, however, objectives focus on the ultimate outcomes required, the ends, managers are free to make the decision which will maximise the likelihood of achieving those outcomes in the face of the new circumstances. Processes and tasks have to be allowed to change when the environment changes.

❏ Robust strategies

At the appraisal stage of the strategic management process, the options need to be subjected to sensitivity testing, to see how the ranking of the options would be affected by different eventualities. This may include comparing the option under different scenarios of the external environment. This sensitivity testing increases understanding of the critical factors, but it should also influence the decisions themselves. It may be decided to choose an option which performs reasonably well however the environment changes in preference to one which performs excellently in the most likely outcome but poorly in other circumstances. Another possibility is to take an interim decision which is compatible with a number of different options and leave final decisions till later, to a time when it could be clearer which way the environment is moving.

Another example of a robust strategy is to build a portfolio of products or a portfolio of suppliers in order to spread the risk. In other words, avoid putting all the eggs in one basket. Relying on a single supplier can make an organisation very dependent on the performance of that supplier; keeping links with other suppliers can make the competition real and give all suppliers the incentive to perform well. On the other hand, good relationships with suppliers can also be important if a change in circumstances means that changes have to be negotiated in contracts with suppliers. This explains in part why many organisations are nowadays seeking to build alliances with key suppliers, rather than keeping suppliers at arm's length in the interests of competition.

Finally, organisations facing uncertainty will often seek to make their own resources flexible. For example, they may prefer to rent property rather than own it, they may decide to employ staff on fixed term contracts and they may seek to employ multi-skilled rather than single skilled people. All of these steps can help to make an organisation better able to cope with unexpected changes.

❑ Contingency plans

It is possible to develop some strategies or action plans which would be brought into play if certain events were to occur. The development of full-blown contingency plans takes staff time and may itself commit certain resources. Therefore they should only normally be prepared for particular risks identified in the analysis and appraisal stages of the strategic management process to be either reasonably likely to materialise or to have extremely severe implications for the business or some combination of both. Such risks could be the loss of a major customer, the destruction of the headquarters building by fire, a catastrophic breakdown of the central computer, or a massive increase in the cost of a major input. For contingency plans to be effective it is vital to be clear:

- what eventuality should trigger the implementation of the plan
- who will be responsible for identifying the need for and authorising the implementation.

Strategic control

Over the last two or three years the concept of strategic control has been much discussed in relation to the public sector, primarily in the context of the relationship between Government departments and executive agencies.

In fact, looking at private sector experience (Goold and Quinn, 1990) suggests that there is no single pattern of control which qualifies as sole owner of the title 'strategic'. The form of control needs to reflect the nature of the business. The only guiding rule is that strategic control must be clearly designed to facilitate the achievement of strategic goals. If some common features have to be identified they would appear to be the following:

- a clear long-term focus shared across all parties
- targets concentrate on progress towards long-term aims and the importance of these targets is reinforced by reward systems
- targets are not dominated by the financial
- shared understanding of the business between all parties.

Where the public sector is concerned, two additional considerations have been added to reflect the particular situation of executive agencies:

- agencies should have a limited number of key targets
- any limitations on the freedom of agencies written into their framework documents should be explicitly justified.

The second of these does not really apply to the private sector, while the first is not always a feature of strategic control systems observed in large corporations.

❑ Long-term focus

Strategic control implies the prior existence of a strategy. In the private sector the concept is applied particularly to relationships between a corporate head-quarters and the company's strategic business units. The controls on those business units are required to move the whole corporation towards its strategic goals. To exercise strategic control, the headquarters must have a corporate strategy to which each of strategic business units contributes. The only exception to this might be a conglomerate where the only common thread between business units is a financial one. In that case, the key targets will only be financial, and it is doubtful whether the concept of strategic control is applicable.

If the idea of strategic control is to be applied to the relationship between Government departments and executive agencies or non-departmental public bodies, the first requirement would appear to be that the department itself has a long-term strategy. Similarly the centre of any organisation cannot really be said to be exercising strategic control over its constituent parts if the organisation does not have a strategy and long-term goals at the corporate level.

❑ Targets linked to the long term

Long-term targets cannot in themselves form the targets for in-year control, nor can they really form the targets for year-to-year control. By the time it is known whether long-term targets have been met, it is too late to make any significant changes to the strategy. Shorter-term targets are therefore essential, but the idea of strategic control is that these targets should be clearly related to the longer-term targets. In effect, they should be readily recognisable as milestones on the road towards the longer-term targets. They may be initiatives or projects, the successful completion of which has been identified as vital to the achievement of longer-term goals. Or, they may be targets which clearly indicate progress towards those goals as, for example, achieving efficiency gains of 4% in two years towards a longer-term target of 9% over 5 years.

❑ Targets not dominated by the financial

Any organisation will have long-term financial goals, but it is likely to have other goals as well. In the private sector, strategic control places considerable, though not exclusive, emphasis on non-financial targets, on achievements regarded as indications of long-term health. In contrast, financial indicators may suggest health, but concentrate on only the current position. Strategic indicators could be items such as market share, customer satisfaction or reliability of the product. If these start to go wrong, financial performance will eventually deteriorate. However, if one waited until a downturn in the financial indicators before taking action, long-term damage may already have been done.

In fact, examination of the current targets of executive agencies and non-departmental public bodies suggests that they are by no means dominated by the financial. However, a further consideration in strategic control is: when there is a conflict between targets, which takes priority? The *spirit* of strategic control implies that the non-financial targets should have equal weight, if not precedence.

❏ Shared understanding

The fourth identified feature of strategic control is a degree of regular contact and shared business understanding between headquarters and the strategic business units. Someone at headquarters will take responsibility for regular liaison with the business units, and monitoring will not simply consist of submission of reports and data to headquarters. It will embrace more frequent discussion of the business, of trends and issues, developing a shared understanding which allows the business unit to take decisions with some confidence that they will be supported by headquarters. In some cases, indeed, strategic control is primarily informal rather than formal. This common understanding also means that targets are not necessarily the be-all and end-all. The targets inevitably are the starting point in any discussion of performance, but, given mutual understanding of the business and of trading conditions, there should be a common understanding of what would constitute good performance in the circumstances as they have turned out.

Use of outside facilitators

If plans are to form a key element in managing a business, they must be owned by all key managers. Thus we have seen the demise of large planning departments in favour of small departments which concentrate on helping managers to do the planning. The planning department provides a framework to manage the planning process, feeds information into the process, offers a necessary element of challenge to proposals, co-ordinates the writing up, and ensures that monitoring systems are in place. If outside consultants are used, they should not be allowed to take ownership of the plan from the managers. This means that they should be used reasonably sparingly.

Outside consultants can make a helpful contribution as facilitators in at least two respects. Firstly, in the early stages of introducing strategic management processes to an organisation, they can offer helpful advice on the essential steps and how they fit together, including advice on which techniques are the more likely to be helpful in that organisation's particular circumstances. They may also be able to offer some technical assistance with the techniques, if they are unfamiliar to the organisation's own staff.

The second role for facilitators is to provide an element of external challenge to the ideas generated internally. This role can be equally valuable for organisations which already have considerable experience of strategic management. Strategic management processes can easily become stale after a time and can benefit from new ideas, new approaches and different techniques. In particular there is a severe danger that mature processes become superficial. There are certainly numerous examples of public sector organisations which have regarded a twenty four hour management board meeting away from the office as sufficient to undertake much of the critical work in developing a plan. This is an assumption which a facilitator may be wary of challenging (for fear of losing the work to a competitor), but a facilitator should certainly challenge:

- views of the world which exhibit complacency
- failure to take views of knowledgeable parties into account.

A facilitator should also be able to ensure that, in any discussion groups, the views of a small minority are not allowed to dominate.

The final health warning is a reminder that, in any purely internal process, a major risk is that all concerned will take a common view of the world, will not wish to challenge each other or may be reticent about challenging the most senior staff, and that the world will be interpreted as the organisation would like it to be rather than as it is. An outside facilitator can help to avoid this. However, a more powerful safeguard should be the collection of as much hard information as possible early in the analysis stage, the use of surveys of stakeholders and customers, and consultation with key parties, including a wide range of the organisation's own staff, at a number of points as plans are developed.

References

Goold, M. and Quinn, J. (1990) *Strategic Control: Milestones for Long-Term Performance* London, The Economist Books.

Chapter 12

Strategic planning in the
Lord Chancellor's Department

The Lord Chancellor's Department (LCD), a central Government department, employing about 11700 civil servants, is responsible for:

- administrative support for the High Court, the Crown Court, the County Courts and certain tribunals
- oversight of the local administration of the magistrates' courts
- funding of, and regulations governing, the legal aid scheme, which is administered by the Legal Aid Board, a non-departmental public body, with the courts remaining responsible for the grant of aid in individual criminal cases
- development of the provision of legal services
- promoting the reform of civil law in England and Wales, on the basis of recommendations from the Law Commission, a non-departmental public body sponsored by LCD
- co-ordinating advice on the appointment of judges, Queen's Counsel, magistrates and tribunal members.

The Department's responsibilities are limited to England and Wales. It took its present shape in 1972, when the Courts Act 1971 gave it the task of administering a reformed court system, comprising the Court of Appeal, the High Court, the Crown Court and the County Courts. Responsibility for the magistrates' courts was transferred from the Home Office to the Lord Chancellor's Department in April 1992.

Figure 12.1 (Cm 2509) shows the Department's expected outturn expenditure in the financial year 1993/94. Of the total expenditure of £2066m, Departmental running costs, basically the costs of Departmental administration, were expected to amount to £404m. Expenditure has been rising in recent years, at about double the rate of general inflation. The largest increase has been in legal aid, 156% since 1988-89.

	£M
Court services	295
Legal aid	1224
Legal aid (administration)	49
Court building programme	106
Salaries of the judiciary	58
Magistrates' courts	
current and capital grants to local authorities	287
credit approvals to local authorities	14
other	33
Total expenditure - Lord Chancellor's Department	2066

Figure 12.1. Lord Chancellor's Department forecast outturn of expenditure 1993/94.

The Lord Chancellor's Department is headed by a Permanent Secretary, who is supported by a management team of three, who take responsibility, respectively, for:

- the court service
- law and policy
- personnel and finance.

The next level below the members of the management team is known as a *group*, then below groups there are *divisions*.

The range of plans

In this account, attention will be focused on the strategic plan and the departmental management plan, but they need to be seen in context. Different plans are produced by different people for different audiences. The categories of plan which will be briefly described are:

- the strategic plan
- the management plan

- divisional plans
- the departmental report
- the court service plan
- the plans of the non-departmental public bodies.

❏ Strategic plan

A strategic plan was produced for the first time in April 1993, and the second was published a year later. The two produced to date have taken a three-year forward look, but consideration is currently being given to changing to a five-year plan. This may or may not be produced annually. The purpose of the strategic plan for 1994/95 to 1996/97 is stated as:

> to enable the Department to develop a long-term and co-ordinated agenda of how best overall to meet and balance the needs of those to whom we are responsible for delivering services. These services may be in the form of properly administered courts, legal services, better law and procedure or other aspects of the law and justice systems.

It deliberately shadows the three-year period of the public expenditure survey, seeking to ensure that arguments about spending requirements are properly justified and to aid prioritisation when pressures on resources change.

While the strategic plan is published and can therefore contribute to the Department's public and parliamentary accountability, to the understanding of all those involved in the administration of justice and to discussions with the Treasury on funding, it is primarily directed towards the Department's own staff. It helps them to understand the general direction and priorities of the Department as defined by the strategic objectives and strategic targets, but it also helps them to put their own work into a wider context. It is a high-level plan, covering Department-wide issues, and provides a framework within which the management plan is prepared.

❏ Management plan

The Departmental management plan is also produced annually and covers the three-year period of the public expenditure survey. The introduction to the plan for the period 1994/95 to 1996/97 describes its role.

> The Management Plan summarises the detailed operational plans of the Department. It describes what individual budget holders are planning to do in order to further the Department's strategic objectives, and the targets they will use to measure their progress.

159

The introduction goes on to emphasise how important it is, if plans are to be delivered, that individual forward job plans should contain objectives which relate to wider corporate objectives, alongside any objectives covering personal development needs.

The management plan is not published, it is essentially an internal document. It is intended primarily for individual budget-holders, setting out the agreed resources and what they have agreed to achieve. It therefore forms the basis for internal monitoring of progress and can also be used, if changes prove to be necessary, to identify the implications of alternative courses of action. The document also goes to the Treasury, who require management plans in connection with their control of running costs. Departments have been required to submit three-year management plans showing how they will achieve efficiency gains, to inform the process of settling spending levels in the public expenditure survey. The LCD management plan, with its internal focus, probably provides more detail than is really necessary for that purpose, covering individual divisions as it does.

❏ Divisional plans

The management plan concentrates on the resources, objectives and targets at divisional level. Some divisions produce their own divisional plan, but this is voluntary. Such plans tend to be confined to a one-year forward look, putting more detail on their entry in the management plan, and identifying specific actions required and the contribution required of individual staff within the division.

❏ Departmental report

The departmental report is a command paper which has to be presented to Parliament early in each calendar year. Each Government department has to present such a report, to explain the department's expenditure plans for the coming three-years, expanding upon the broader figures announced by the Chancellor of the Exchequer in the budget statement the previous November. This report is therefore primarily a public document, a requirement of Parliamentary and public accountability. Its content is determined in part by Parliamentary requirements and by the Treasury; every department is required to include some common elements in a common format. The report explains:

- where the money has been spent over the previous four years and where it will be spent over the coming three-years
- major polices and initiatives
- past and planned performance, on the basis of a number of performance indicators, covering levels of service, productivity and unit cost, and workload.

The departmental report represents the first statement of plans following confirmation of the resources available. Inevitably there is considerable duplication between the departmental report and the strategic and management plans, but the report is required for a different audience and for a specific purpose of Parliamentary and public accountability.

❏ Plans of the Court Service and non-departmental public bodies

The Court Service is due to become an executive agency on 1 April 1995. This means that it will need to start to produce its own strategic and business plans. The Court Service will be resourced by the Lord Chancellor's Department and its plans will therefore need both to contribute to, and to reflect, LCD plans. The same situation currently applies to the non-departmental public bodies sponsored by LCD.

Organisation of, and involvement in, planning

There are two different parts of the Lord Chancellor's Department which have some specific responsibilities for leading and co-ordinating the planning effort. They are:

- Central Unit
- Resources Division.

The Central Unit takes responsibility for strategic planning, while Resources Division puts together the management plan and the departmental report.

❏ Central Unit

The Central Unit is currently located within the command of the management team member responsible for law and policy. The Unit's objectives embrace:

- developing and operating systems to enable senior management to set strategic direction
- monitoring the delivery of strategic objectives
- communication and information strategies, systems and services
- carrying through central initiatives
- assurance that systems are in place to ensure value for money in the use of staff and other resources.

Current responsibilities covered by these objectives include establishing an analytical capability to support policy development, advice on objectives and performance indicators, management and organisational arrangements for information and information technology strategies, review of requirements for statistical services, planning and implementation of an information systems network, achieving of savings from a specific initiative in library services, market testing, a specific initiative in the equal opportunities area, and implementation of workload measurement. The Central Unit as a whole has a staff of about 80, but within that the responsibility for facilitating and co-ordinating the strategic planning process is covered by less than two full-time equivalents. The person with lead responsibility also acts as secretary to the Management Board and therefore has regular direct access to top management in general and the Permanent Secretary in particular.

❏ Resources Division

Resources Division is located within the command of the Principal Establishment and Finance Officer. The responsibilities of Resources Division include:

- producing the annual end year accounts, the appropriation account
- preparation of the annual estimates of the cash requirements (the vote), for approval by Parliament and then monitoring and control of actual expenditure
- coordination of the Department's contribution to the public expenditure survey (PES)
- allocation of the vote and approved public expenditure within the Department
- charging mechanisms
- banking arrangements.

Staffing of the Division amounts to about 40 people, but again the staffing devoted specifically to facilitating the management planning process is very limited, amounting probably to little more than one full-time equivalent. The main effort falls on line managers, particularly at about Grade 5 level, the Division heads.

❏ Separation of responsibilities for strategic and management planning

Management planning has been established for some time. When strategic planning was set up more recently, it was a deliberate intention that strategic planning should be distinct from management planning. It was felt important that strategic planning should not be, and should be clearly seen not to be, dominated by financial considerations. While financial matters must be recognised within strategic planning, strategy has to embrace a wider perspective of purpose and direction.

In the case of management planning, the link with financial matters is much more direct. Resources have to be secured through the public expenditure survey, and the allocation of resources must both inform the Department's negotiations during that survey and reflect the settlement reached. The plan must also form the basis for monitoring and control of resources in-year, to ensure that expenditure is kept within the limits approved by Parliament. Having said that, though, there must be links between the management plan and the strategy. The securing and allocation of resources must seek to move the Department in the direction agreed in the strategic plan. Good working relationships between the Central Unit and Resources Division are therefore important. The link has to be particularly strong in the preparation of the Departmental Report, where there is a major input from those who co-ordinate the strategic planning.

Consistency between the strategic plan and the management plan is ensured in part by finalising them together, at the same time of year. The link between the two is also made clear in the management plan by making explicit links between strategic objectives and operational objectives. At Divisional level, each operational objective is accompanied by a reference to the strategic objective to which it contributes. In addition, alongside each strategic objective is a complete list of the operational objectives which support it.

There are plans for some reorganisation of Divisions within the Department to reflect the creation of the Court Service Agency. This will involve moving the responsibility for strategic planning to the command of the Principal Establishment and Finance Officer. However, although under the same command, it will remain separate from Resources Division, so there will still be a separation of responsibilities for strategic planning and for management planning. This emphasises the importance attached to a non-financial perspective in strategic planning.

❏ Consultation and involvement

Responsibilities within the planning process will become clearer subsequently when the process is described in more detail. The strategic plan is currently primarily a top-down exercise, deliberately so because of the desire to identify key issues and challenges across the Department. In contrast, the management plan is primarily bottom-up, with Groups and Divisions taking the lead in proposing their own objectives and targets. The Management Board is closely involved at all key stages, right through to their consideration of quarterly monitoring reports of progress against strategic objectives and targets. In the preparation of the strategic plan staff down to Grade 5, basically Division heads, are formally consulted and some become more directly involved by preparing papers for consideration. The main strategic planning conference comprises about 20 staff, the Management Board, most of the Grade 3 staff, broadly heads of Groups, plus some staff at Grade 5. There will then be further discussion between the strategic planning staff and individual staff on particular issues as the strategic plan is finalised over a period of about six months.

In contrast, the lead in preparing the details of the management plan lies primarily with staff at about Grade 5 level. The proposals come from individual heads of Groups and of Divisions. Each person will have his or her own approach to this. Many will involve their staff in the process, but there are no set rules.

The planning process

The key elements of the planning process are:

- review of the process in the previous year and preparation of key papers
- strategic planning conference
- finalising the strategies and writing of the strategic plan
- preparation and agreement of the operational objectives and targets for the management plan
- monitoring.

❏ Review and preparation

The strategic planning cycle begins in the early part of the financial year, in April or May, with a review of the experience of the process in the previous year. This review will cover both the process itself and the actual course of events and their implications for the strategy. This is a period when senior staff are encouraged to think about the future. In particular, in July there is a conference for all staff at Grade 5 in the Department. The conference is an opportunity to identify themes and issues which concern people and which will need to be addressed in the strategic plan. An outcome will be commissioning of papers on these important issues for the September conference.

❏ The September conference

The conference is a key, perhaps the key, event in the strategic planning calendar. It lasts two days and, in the light of the papers provided, seeks to confirm the foundations of the plan and to prepare an outline of it. The conference follows a carefully structured agenda, which has been discussed with, and agreed, by the Management Board. The use of a structured agenda ensures that the themes agreed by the Management Board to be important are addressed and that progress is made in resolving those issues.

❏ Finalising the strategies

After the September conference, the small strategic planning unit tends to become the focal point for further progress. The outline agreed by the conference needs to be fleshed out. Some issues will require further work, ideas will need to be firmed up and then discussed with those across the Department who have an interest. The strategic planners take the lead in commissioning the necessary work, in ensuring appropriate consultation and in preparing drafts for the agreement of the Management Board. During this period the public expenditure survey outcome will become clear, in November, and the impact of this will need to be reflected in the strategy, although in practice the impact is primarily at the operational or management plan level.

❏ Preparing the management plan

The agreements reached at the September conference provide an appropriate backcloth against which the bottom-up planning can commence. The public expenditure survey settlement announced at the end of November is, however, a vital input to this process. If the settlement is very different from the figure expected, there will be a need for further guidance on priorities. The proposed Divisional and Group plans submitted to Resources Division set out the resources required for the coming three-years, pay costs, other running costs, non-running costs and manpower numbers. Resources Division have to ensure that the aggregate is contained within the total resources allocated to the Department and that the distribution is in line with the Department's strategy and agreed priorities. The process will reach a conclusion in about April, at the same time as the strategic plan, and both plans should be agreed by the Management Board together.

❏ Monitoring

In the introductory paragraphs of the management plan, it is pointed out that it is a tool to allow individual managers to monitor their Division's performance and progress throughout the year. It is proposed that, from next year, the management plan should include a section showing performance against the prior year's targets. Resources Division will monitor expenditure of Divisions regularly throughout the year. The Management Board, however, has, since April 1993, received a regular quarterly bulletin, which focuses its attention on progress against the targets in the strategic plan and against related key measures of performance. The Management Board also has a rolling programme of stewardship reports, covering progress at Group level over the previous 12 months.

The format of plans

In reviewing the format of the written documents, it is important to remember that each plan is produced with a different audience in mind:

- the Departmental report is produced for Parliament and the general public, though the direct readership will inevitably be confined largely to professional commentators
- the strategic plan is a published document, and, while it says that it is primarily directed towards staff, it is intended to be useful to a wider audience, particularly the large number of people outside the Department who are involved in the administration of justice
- the management plan is an unpublished document, internal to the Department; designed to be circulated to all managers, it is described as a vehicle for cascading plans down the management chain and disseminating them widely within the Department.

❏ The strategic plan

To date, formal analytical techniques have not featured strongly in the formulation of the strategic plan. When strategic planning was first started, a SWOT analysis was undertaken to help to identify the issues which needed to be addressed. The strategic planning unit also produced a PEST paper for consultation with interested parties, to establish key assumptions about external trends and developments. Further, such structured thinking techniques are likely to be used in future to take maximum advantage of the involvement of senior staff in the planning process.

The written document contains five major elements:

- foundations
- key challenges with strategic objectives and documents
- plans for the future
- facts and figures
- progress against plan.

Foundations

The foundations consist of a fundamental aim, a strategic priority and some guiding principles. These were developed prior to the introduction of strategic planning and are thus an input to rather than an output from the strategic planning process. The fundamental aim is:

> to ensure the efficient and effective administration of justice at an affordable cost.

The strategic priority is to control legal aid costs and contain expenditure on court services, while maintaining proper standards of service. The guiding principles are:

- to protect and advance the rule of law
- to ensure a fair and efficient system of justice
- to safeguard the independence of the judiciary and the judicial process
- to provide service to all citizens using or involved in the processes of the law
- to ensure openness, subject only to exceptions necessary to protect individuals and the public interest
- to promote equal opportunities.

Key challenges

The heart of the strategic planning process is to identify the key challenges which run across the whole of the Department's responsibilities and to reach agreement on the strategic objectives and targets which follow from them. The written plan is about 40 pages in length and the challenges, objectives and targets take about half of that. The text only states what the challenges, objectives and targets are, it does not describe the process by which they were derived, or the reasoning behind them. The key challenges admirably illustrate the notion of 'strategic issues' described in Chapter 3, taking the form of issues where the ultimate objective is clear, but there are options as to how the objective will be delivered. The key challenges are:

- to ensure access to justice while reducing its cost to the parties and the taxpayer
- to sustain improvements in the quality, efficiency and effectiveness of court services
- to gain control of the overall cost of legal aid while ensuring an adequate level of publicly funded legal services

- to support improvements in the appointment and training of the judiciary
- to develop a range of policies which contribute to the protection of the rights of the individual, the family and property and, where appropriate, to support these policies with an effective law reform process
- to build structures and mechanisms, within planned levels of resources, to enable the Department to meet its key challenges and carry out its other functions.

Under each key challenge there is then a set of between two and six strategic objectives, of which the following are examples which illustrate the general style:

- to enable parties to resolve their disputes more speedily
- to secure the availability of an increasing a range of advisory and representational services
- to distribute courts and centres for resolving disputes to optimise access to justice
- to control unit costs in the Court Service and magistrates' courts
- to hold the overall cost of legal aid to planned levels
- to carry forward the programme announced by the Lord Chancellor in July 1993 for reforms in the arrangements for appointing the judiciary
- to establish a coherent, fairer and simpler body of law
- to deploy and manage the Department's financial resources to best effect.

Each strategic objective is then backed by up to four targets, which help to tighten up on the meaning of the strategic objectives. The targets tend not to be numerical, though there are a few which are implicitly numerical, for example:

to contain the unit cost growth in legal aid remuneration so that by March 1996 it does not exceed inflation.

In some cases, they are more specific about the ultimate outcome required. For example, the objective of increasing the range of advisory and representational services is supported by a target:

to increase the number and variety of ways of providing legal services by December 1995.

Many of the targets describe particular initiatives and actions to be taken and completed by specific dates. Examples are:

to introduce a scheme for graduated fees for advocates in the Crown Court by October 1994 and a scheme for standardised fees for litigators for civil work by January 1995

to compete the initial stage of the Fundamental Review of the legal aid scheme by June 1994

to secure, by July 1994, Management Board agreement to the reorganisation of headquarters

to provide a single code of procedural rules for the High Court and County Courts by beginning of April 1997.

Plans for the future

This section, covering about ten pages of the strategic plan, is in a more narrative form. For example, it explains more about the measures announced by the Lord Chancellor in July 1993 for improving procedures for judicial appointments. It also says more about the objectives for legal aid and the proposals for gaining control of the overall cost. The emphasis in this section is on expanding on the steps and procedures underlying the objectives and targets rather than on explicit justification of the choice of objectives, targets and priorities.

Facts and figures

This section of the plan is purely factual, without any narrative or explanation. Items included are:

- organisation chart
- allocation of resources, between court services, court buildings, magistrates' courts, legal aid, judicial salaries
- judicial numbers
- distribution of staff, between headquarters, County Courts, Crown Court, Public Trust Office, and so on
- workload trends, cases, petitions, warrants, committals, sittings.

Progress against plan

The final section of the strategic plan is a brief narrative of what has been achieved in the past twelve months, with a section covering each of the strategic objectives. The narrative includes a good deal of numerical information on items such as speed of dealing with cases, courtroom utilisation, backlogs of work.

Communication

The strategic plan, as a published document, is widely available without charge.

Within the Department, a leaflet is produced, summarising the plan, and circulated to the more junior staff, at Executive Officer and below. A full copy of the plan is available in each branch of the Department and in each individual court. When the plan was produced, it was distributed to all circuit administrators within the courts' service, together with a question and answer brief.

Assessment

The content and presentation of the document clearly reflects its target audience. It is a 'glossy' document, professionally produced, but not so glossy as to appear primarily a public relations document. The key challenges, strategic objectives and targets clearly identify it as a working document as well.

❏ Management plan

The management plan is very clearly a working document, with three sections:

- introduction
- links to the strategic plan
- operational plans.

Out of a total of 79 pages, the first section covers two pages, the second four pages.

Introduction

The introduction briefly describes the link between the strategic plan and the management plan, the role of the management plan in particular, its format, and intentions for the future development of the management plan.

> The Management Plan summarises the detailed operational plans of the various parts of the Department. It describes what individual budget holders are planning to do in order to further the Department's strategic objectives, and the targets they will use to measure their progress. It is essential to establish clear links between the high level aims and objectives of the organisation as a whole and the day-to-day work of individual offices and staff. The Management Plan provides that link by setting out budget holders' objectives which should contribute to the achievement of one or more of the Department's strategic objectives.

Links to the strategic plan

This section of the management plan is primarily tabular in form. Each key challenge is reproduced, then under each challenge the appropriate strategic objectives, together with the operational objectives which support it, in the form illustrated by the examples shown in Figure 12.2.

Strategic objectives	Division/Business area	Operational objectives
1.1 Reduce cost of resolving disputes	PL1 Legal Services, etc PL2 Legal Aid PL3 Family Law CS1 Criminal Business	1.1 2.2 2.4 3.1 3.2 1.5 1.7 1.8
5.3 Establish a coherent and simpler body of law	L1 Law Reform PL3 Family Law Law Commission	1.1 3.1 3.2 3.3 3.4 3.6 1.1 1.2 1.3
6.2 Reorganise for Court Service Agency	CU Central Unit EF3 Resources Division	1.1 3.3

Figure 12.2. Examples of link of strategic and operational objectives.

Operational plans

The section containing the operational plans includes no narrative at all, it simply records the resources, operational objectives and operational targets which have been agreed for the three-years ahead, together with a statement against each operational objective identifying the strategic objective to which it contributes. The objectives tend to be statements of general purpose and direction. While the targets sometimes specify numerical levels of performance to achieve, more often they identify specific tasks by specific dates to move in the direction implied by the objective. Some examples are given in Figure 12.3.

Operational objectives	Operational targets
To improve drafting and organisation of rules and regulations	(i) Establish common code of procedural rules by July 1995. (ii) Introduce plain English code for small claims by October 1994.
To consolidate discrete areas of statute law	(i) Consolidate not less than five areas of statute law per annum.
To devise systems of payment for legal aid which achieve better control over the quality of service and unit costs of legal aid, and which provide value for money	(i) Introduce system of graduated fees in Crown Court (advocates) by October 1994. (ii) Introduce system of standard fees for solicitors for civil cases by January 1995. (iii) Introduce payment schemes for solicitors (non-advocacy) work in Crown Court during 1995-96. (iv) Develop and implement payment systems for barristers doing civil work during 1995-96. (v) Develop and implement mechanisms for obtaining information about cost and cost drivers of civil cases by December 1994. (vi) Ensure standard fees cover 85% of volume of legal aid work and 60% of total expenditure by March 1995.

Figure 12.3. Examples of operational objectives and targets.

The management plan states that, next year, the plan will additionally include a section to show actual performance against the previous year's plan.

Assessment

At present, the strategic plan is distinguished from the management plan primarily by the level at which attention is directed. Both plans have a three-year forward horizon. In many respects, the strategic plan has introduced an appropriate element of top-down planning to what could otherwise be an entirely bottom-up system. The strategic plan identifies Department-wide issues and objectives, initially in draft form, which serve as guidance to Divisions for the preparation of their own plans. The top-down and bottom-up elements are then brought together and finalised at broadly the same time.

When the first strategic plan was prepared, there were some thoughts that it duplicated the management plan. There was a tendency to try to develop the strategic objectives by building them up from the operational objectives which already existed. This just illustrates the difficulty in standing back from currently agreed activities to identify fundamental issues which could lead to a change in priorities. In the second strategic planning exercise, it was felt that real progress was made in identifying and focusing on issues, such as access to justice at affordable cost, which had not previously been recognised as explicitly and which now are exerting influence on the operational objectives.

Now that some experience has been gained of strategic planning, thought is being given to:

- whether the process needs to be repeated annually
- whether the horizon should be raised to, perhaps, five years rather than three
- the need to reflect the creation of the Court Service Agency.

The longer horizon would help to draw a clearer distinction between the strategic plan and the management plan, and may make it easier to stand back from existing activities to identify more strategic issues. However, the bottom-up management plan would still need to be supported by a top-down element, to identify key themes and corporate targets for the three-year period. This might be provided by a review of progress made to date against the current strategic plan.

❏ The data base

One of the problems encountered in the early years of strategic planning has been the lack of data to support the process. This is hardly surprising because the data requirements only become evident as planning proceeds. While data have been collected over the years on trends in workloads, there is insufficient information on why trends change, insufficient understanding of the factors which will affect the demands on the Department. At present, it is felt that there is probably too much reliance on discussion and not enough on hard data, and to that end one of the operational objectives is to build an analytical unit to help inform strategic and policy debate and decisions within the Department.

❏ Strategic plan as a management tool

Again, it will take time for the strategic plan to be recognised as a tool which can be used to guide and inform decisions throughout the year. For example, there has been experience of a need to make cost savings in-year as a result of receipts turning out to be lower than expected. The strategic plan should provide an opportunity to review the options against the impact on the key challenges. However, it is not a straightforward exercise to relate resources to key challenges, and there may still be a tendency to look first to more traditional methods of finding emergency savings, such as across-the-board reductions. The strategic planning process will need to be developed to make it easier to use in these situations. At the same time, some effort will need to be devoted to raising awareness that the plan can be used in this way. There is already evidence that senior managers are relating their consideration of policy proposals to the key challenges, for example, what will the proposal do for access to justice?

❏ Staff commitment

To staff below the level of head of Division, the relevance of the strategic plan will be felt through its impact on their own objectives. The link with Divisional objectives, in the management plan, is clear, but it is now intended to move forward with trying to link individual objectives and forward job plans to the Divisional objectives.

To quote the management plan:

> The Department's objectives are delivered by the efforts of individuals. It is therefore important that individuals' personal objectives should reflect the contribution which they will make to the achievement of the wider operational and strategic objectives of the organisation. Senior managers in the Department are currently looking to set standards to ensure the Forward Job Plans contain objectives based on wider corporate plans, as well as more personal development objectives.

❏ Fundamental expenditure reviews

As a contribution towards the control of public expenditure in the longer term, Government departments are required to undertake fundamental reviews of areas of expenditure agreed with the Treasury. These are, in effect, strategic studies of particular activities. The reviews have to be undertaken fairly hurriedly, to fit the timetable of the public expenditure survey. As a result, they have to be undertaken outside the normal strategic planning process. Clearly, the outcome of these reviews, which in the case of the Lord Chancellor's Department will cover areas such as legal aid, civil justice and the court building programme, will have to be integrated into the strategic plan. It seems likely that the experience of these reviews will influence the Department's approach to strategic planning, perhaps encouraging a longer time horizon and the development of a more analytical approach.

Further reading

Cm 2509 (1994) *Departmental Report of the Lord Chancellor's and Law Officers' Departments* London, HMSO

Lord Chancellor's Department (1994) *A Programme for the Future: Strategic Plan 1994/95 - 1996/97* London, HMSO

Chapter 13

Corporate planning at the Countryside Commission

The Countryside Commission is a non-departmental public body (an NDPB), which was created by statute in 1968 as a direct successor to the National Parks Commission. The focus of the new Commission was broadened to embrace the countryside as a whole. Its main statutory responsibilities are:

- the designation of Areas of Outstanding Natural Beauty
- to be a statutory consultee in planning and development control
- the promotion of understanding and enjoyment through informing the public of their rights and responsibilities in the countryside
- advice to the Capital Taxes Office on inheritance tax exemptions
- the designation of National Parks and advice to the Secretary of State on nominations to National Park Authorities
- the development of National Trails
- advice to water companies on the consideration of conservation and recreation interests in their disposal of land, and the negotiation of covenants on behalf of the Secretary of State where appropriate.

Current themes and activities include:

- conserving and enhancing our most valued landscapes through working with National Park Authorities, supporting Areas of Outstanding Natural Beauty and Heritage Coasts, Countryside Stewardship and Hedgerow Incentive schemes and a programme of restoration of historic parks and gardens
- enhancing poor landscapes, through the Community Forests programme, the creation of a National Forest, specific countryside management projects, and working with Groundwork Trusts who tackle derelict and neglected land
- improving access to and enjoyment of the countryside, through working with highway authorities on rights of way, including National Trails, and access elements of, for example, Community Forests and the National Forest

- promoting public involvement in the countryside, through education and training, Rural Action partnerships and support to the voluntary sector.

This list of activities is far from exhaustive but it gives some idea of the breadth of work.

It should be emphasised that the Countryside Commission owns no land and does not itself operate facilities or provide services directly to the general public. It works primarily through others. Total staffing numbers about 300, with planned expenditure of about £46m in the financial year 1994/95. The source of funding is virtually entirely grant-in-aid received through the Department of the Environment, the Commission's sponsoring department. The expenditure of £46m is expected to be broken down as shown in Figure 13.1. The high percentage of expenditure allocated to third parties illustrates the extent to which the Countryside Commission works through others. The Commission has set a 25% ceiling on its total internal costs, all other funds are devoted to action.

	£M
Salaries	6.8
Administrative expenses	3.6
Research and experiment	2.0
Publicity and information	1.3
Grants	31.8
Other	0.6
Total	46.1

Figure 13.1. Planned financial allocations 1994/95.

The organisation of the Commission is shown in Figure 13.2. The eight members of the Commission, including the chairman, are appointed by the Secretary of State for the Environment. The senior management team, which meets weekly, consists of the Director General plus the three Divisional Directors. Each Director also holds regular meetings of his own team. It will be seen from the organisation chart that the operations group is regionally based but that there are also some special units which have an interest across all regions. The policy group includes research activities. The resources group essentially provides central support services. In addition to the relationships shown on the organisation chart, there are currently five Cross-Divisional Groups, each chaired by one of the Directors, which cover key areas of work which cut across divisional boundaries. These groups report back formally to the senior management team. The operations division also has special subject teams, each normally chaired by a Regional Officer (head of a regional office) to ensure an appropriate degree of common practice across the regions. The person chairing the subject team would normally also be a member of any related Cross-Divisional Group.

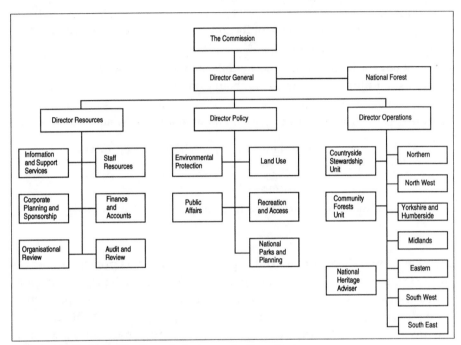

Figure 13.2. Countryside Commission organisation chart.

The hierarchy of plans

The published Corporate Plan is currently the highest level output of the Countryside Commission's corporate planning process. Other key elements in the process are:

- branch or regional management plans
- business plans
- value for money studies
- implementation programmes
- individual work programmes, or forward job plans.

A first strategic plan, known as the Commission's 'Prospectus', was approved by the Commissioners in August 1994.

❏ The corporate plan

The corporate plan is produced annually and looks four years ahead. The plan is finalised in the Spring and the four-year period has been deliberately chosen so that:

- it can reflect the outcome of the public expenditure survey completed the previous Autumn
- it covers the period of, and can inform, the three-year public expenditure survey which is about to commence.

The three main purposes of the corporate plan, according to the staff handbook, are:

a.   to plan and guide our work and get value for money from our limited funds and small staff;

b.   to explain to our partners what we aim to do;

c.   to make the case for supporting our work to Government and others.

The plan is published, but whilst it is publicly available its primary audiences are the Department of the Environment and the Commission's partners. It opens with a brief statement of overall strategy, then identifies some principal themes for the planning period. However, the main emphasis is on the allocation of resources to programmes and on the key targets, mostly in the form of tasks or actions for completion, for each programme. In the plan for 1994/95 to 1997/98 there were in total 28 separate programmes, the description of which covered about 30 pages of the total of 50 in the plan. The contents of these descriptions are explained later.

The programmes run across the divisional groupings and are therefore particularly valuable in relating expenditure to objectives and priorities, for the Commission's own staff, partners and Government. The structure of the plan clearly reflects the declared purposes of the plan.

❏ Branch or regional management plans

All branches and regions are required to produce their own management plans as part of the corporate planning exercise. These also have a four-year horizon, and both inform and support the Corporate Plan. They are prepared in draft in a common format in the Autumn, after the September conference, and are then made firmer when the grant-in-aid settlement is known. These branch and regional plans, in an interactive process, both contribute to, and reflect, the ideas incorporated in the plans for programme areas set out in the corporate plan. The final versions will have to be consistent with the final version of the corporate plan.

Up until 1994/95, only the branches and regions within the Policy and Operations Divisions produced management plans, but the requirement has now been widened to incorporate branches within Resources Division as well.

❑ Business plans

Business plans are individual one-off exercises, prepared to consider and make the case for a major new initiative. In most cases the need for an initiative is flagged up initially in a management plan. The senior management team would then signal the requirement for a business plan. These plans will cover initiatives which run across branch or regional boundaries, and each plan will cover one initiative only. They may be used solely for internal purposes, or they may be used as submissions to Government, to seek approval for the initiative. In essence they ensure that the resource requirements and impact across the Commission are considered fully *before* a commitment is made to take the work forward.

❑ Implementation programmes

Implementation programmes are, like business plans, prepared for areas of work which cut across branches and regions. They are, however, few in number and confined to particularly large areas of work, such as the Commission's involvement in planning (town and country planning) issues. The intention is to ensure cohesion in a more detailed way than would be appropriate to the corporate plan itself.

❑ Individual foward job plans

Individual forward job plans and work programmes are seen as an essential element of the corporate planning process. These job plans look one year ahead, and performance against them is appraised every six months. Responsibility for setting individual objectives rests clearly with line managers. Forward job plans provide the fine detail for the management plans.

The planning process

The corporate planning and sponsorship group is located within Resources Division, as shown in Figure 13.2. The group also has responsibility for raising commercial sponsorship to support the Commission's programmes and initiatives. There is always a query as to whether planning would be more logically located within Policy Division, but its present location reflects the importance of the plan for securing and allocating resources. The planning process is key to making the case to Government for grant-in-aid, as will be explained later in the chapter.

The corporate planning unit consists of five people, headed at Civil Service Grade 7 level. The other four members of the group are a Senior and a Higher Executive Officer, an Executive Officer and an Administrative Officer. The Senior Executive Officer post has been a temporary one specifically to develop the new strategy (prospectus). These posts are trawled within the Commission, so that interest in the work is assured. The essential qualities for the senior posts in planning are considered to be:

- an understanding of how things work right across the Commission
- a knowledge of how to find information
- good inter-personal relationships.

The present corporate planning process is shown in Figure 13.3 and described below in six stages:

- initial analysis
- top-down guidelines
- bottom-up proposals
- finalisation of the plan
- submission to and discussion with Government
- monitoring.

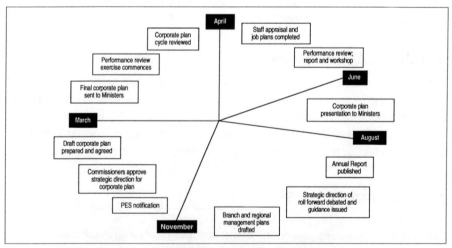

Figure 13.3. Countryside Commission: the corporate planning cycle.

❏ Initial analysis

As suggested in Chapter 3, planning should be a continuous process, and it is therefore often difficult to know where to break into the cycle to start describing it. In the case of the Countryside Commission, our description starts with the performance review, which serves jointly as the close of one planning cycle and the opening of the next. This review takes place in April and May each year and aims to give the Commission information on its performance against the targets it set for the financial year which has just finished. Individual branches and regional officers gather data on the volumes of activity achieved and on the progress being made on projects. As from 1994/95 all cost centres are required to produce their report in a common format. The information gathered is then consolidated by the corporate planning group into a single internal document in mid-May. This serves three purposes:

- it provides a basis for the Commission's Annual Report which is published in September
- it may lead to adjustments for the targets for the current year, that is the first year of the Corporate Plan which has been finalised a month or so before
- it serves as a major element of the analysis stage for the new plan, identifying where performance is strong or weak, where circumstances have changed, which customers have been best or worst served, and so on.

In recent years the performance review document has, for each programme, listed the objectives and targets and then, on the facing page, a statement on whether the target was achieved or on the extent to which it was achieved. This year the review has adopted a narrative format, with a statement on each programme, including some explanations of successes and failures and assessments of the implications.

During the month or two after completion of the performance review, the corporate planning group aim to hold three or four meetings with staff at Grade 7 level across the Commission. These will mostly be heads of branches or regions. The purpose of the meetings, ideally led by the senior management team, is to debate key areas of performance, debate which informs the planning group in their preparation of planning guidelines to put to the senior management team for approval. In the past, these meetings have been used to try to discuss strategic issues and strategic options ab initio, but in practice this has not proved particularly helpful. It has been difficult to stand back from the present position, and debate has tended to revert to building up or cutting back from current activity. As explained later, in the section headed 'assessment', the Commission has highly committed, professional staff, and there is also strong political commitment to many of the things which it does. This makes it difficult to consider major strategic change outside the context of a more overtly and explicitly strategic review.

❑ Top-down guidelines

The performance review and the meetings with staff at Grade 7 level inform the corporate planning group in their preparation of some draft strategic guidelines. During this period there will also be feedback from meetings with Department of the Environment officials and the Minister about the previous corporate plan. Consideration also has to be given to the impact of any recent Government decisions, such as the outcome of the review of the Sports Council, the Forestry Review, and so on. The planning group also makes a positive effort during this period to talk to key people and take their views. The guidelines are initially presented to the senior management team in the form of a series of questions. These questions are debated by the management team and views are reached. These views are then incorporated into the strategic guidance which:

- identifies key themes
- suggests which areas of activity should grow or decline or be subject to a change of emphasis
- stipulates key assumptions
- sets out the timetable for the further stages of planning and a common format for the presentation of data.

The guidance is then issued to the branches and regions in October when draft management plans are commissioned.

❑ Bottom-up proposals

Once the strategic guidance has been circulated, the main focus moves to the heads of branches and regions. They are required to submit draft plans by the end of November. Although there is a common format for the presentation of key data, there is no central prescription as to how the management plans are prepared, so the procedures will tend to reflect the styles of individual managers. The links between the management plans and forward job plans do tend to encourage staff participation in preparing plans, as does the fact that a good deal of detailed knowledge resides below the level of branch or regional head. It is known that some of the heads hold major planning meetings.

The management plans are submitted in the first instance to the three Divisional Directors, so that they can reconcile divisional priorities before the plans go to the corporate planning group. This step was introduced last year for the first time, and has helped to achieve more consistency between the plans. Directors can themselves hold meetings with their branch heads at the start of the management planning process to agree divisional priorities and facilitate a higher degree of consistency between the individual plans eventually produced.

❏ Finalisation of the plan

When the draft plans have been submitted, the corporate planning group becomes the centre of activity. The group has to go through the individual plans to check for duplication, overlap, inconsistencies between plans, inconsistencies with the original guidance. They will also need to consider the implications of the grant-in-aid settlement for the proposals submitted.

There may be a good deal of discussion with branch and regional heads to check details during this period, the purpose being to clarify issues, not really to resolve them. The issues are then put to the senior management team for resolution.

Proposals made by the senior management team are then put to a meeting of the Commissioners in February for their approval. When that approval has been given, the corporate planning group proceeds to prepare the final written version of the plan. Branch Heads and Regional Officers then adjust their management plans in the light of the Commission's decisions.

❏ Submissions to and discussion with Government

The final version of the plan is completed by the end of March, approved by the Chairman, and then formally submitted to the Minister. A draft will have been shown a little earlier to officials of the Department of the Environment for informal feedback. This helps to identify any elements which could need further explanation or which conflict with developments known to be occurring elsewhere. There is also a formal meeting between the Director General and Departmental Officials, which the head of the corporate planning group attends. This acts as a shadow meeting to that between the Chairman and the Minister. The Chairman of the commission meets formally with the Minister to discuss the plan and any key messages from this meeting are then fed back into the analysis stage of the following corporate plan, which has been explained above. The head of the corporate planning group also attends the meeting with the Minister.

The submission of the plan to the Department of the Environment at the end of March is timed to allow the Department to reflect the proposals in the plan in its own contribution to the public expenditure survey starting in May. To that end, the Commission is required to submit information on the implications if grant-in-aid figures were 10% higher or lower than the planning figures on which the plan is based. The implications of 10% increases or reductions in financing are published in the Corporate Plan. To inform this exercise, programmes are prioritised, an analysis which enables the Commission to adjust much more rapidly to the actual grant-in-aid settlement when it is announced than would otherwise be the case.

❏ Monitoring

Every quarter, a resources report is presented to the senior management team. This covers expenditure by programme area. Although individual staff appraisal has been undertaken every six months, it has only been possible in the past to report progress formally against objectives at corporate level annually. This reflects in part the nature of the objectives, which do not lend themselves to assessment in a straightforward numerical way. In the future, a new system will permit the production of quarterly cost centre reports of outturns against budget for each cost centre and at the same time embrace performance against other objectives.

Format of the corporate plan

The corporate plan for 1994/95 to 1997/98, after an executive summary, consists of the following sections:

- introduction
- performance review
- strategy
- programme
- management and organisation
- appendices.

Before looking at the content of each in turn, it is worth bearing in mind the audience for the plan.

❏ The audience

A copy of the corporate plan is sent to every member of staff. Copies are also distributed to major partners or to groups representative of the partners, for example, voluntary bodies, English Nature, local authority associations.

Summaries may be produced by Regional offices for local distribution but as yet there is no common format or practice.

To aid the internal communication process, it is intended in future to visit the regions to explain the plan and to hold workshops on it. Information about the plan is also communicated through a network bulletin board. However, the plan also has a large external audience. Its role in relation to this audience is explained in the Commission's staff handbook.

> The Plan's role in relation to partners is especially important because the Commission achieves its objectives almost exclusively through the work of others. The Plan is the basis of any 'prospectus' the Commission wants to show off to potential partners what its aims, objectives and programmes are. Collaborators can decide where their activities might fit in and Commission staff can forge alliances with them that will achieve both the Ccommission's objectives and the aspirations of the collaborator.

> The Plan's role in relation to Government is also crucial. Current Government practice for Non-departmental Public Bodies is to allocate grant-in-aid and approve staff resources on the basis of the targets and resource requirements set out in annual corporate plans. The grant-in-aid relationship with Government therefore demands that the Commission produces a corporate plan each year. Under present government practice, it is a useful concept to view the Commission's corporate plan as a grant application which becomes our contract with the Department of the Environment, undertaking to achieve certain targets in return for public money allocated.

❏ Introduction

The introduction is quite brief, only one page in length. It starts with an explanation of the role of the plan. Then it describes the key assumptions. These largely concern the activities for which the Commission will retain responsibility, but there is also an assumption that staff and support costs in 1994/95 will be held at 1993/94 outturn levels. Finally, three key uncertainties are identified:

- a possible merger with English Nature, a study of which has been requested by the Secretary of State
- local government reorganisation and stringency in local authority finance
- the workload involved in advising the National Heritage Memorial Fund in relation to the National Lottery.

The implication is that, if any of these eventualities materialise, amendments to the plan will be necessary.

❏ Performance review

Performance in 1993/94 is reviewed on each of four main themes and on management and organisation. This section, covering two pages, is extremely factual, describing activities, including volumes of some activities in numerical terms, tasks undertaken and completed, and some disappointments. It cannot really go into analysis of reasons for successes and failures and their implications for planning. This is because the plan is written in February and March, but the final review cannot be undertaken until April and May, after the year end. This section in the plan therefore has to be a preliminary and indicative view.

❏ Strategy

Reference is made to the preparation of a new strategy, and we shall return to that below in the section entitled 'Assessment'. Although a formal longer-term strategic plan has not been prepared in the past, this does not mean that there has been no attempt to think strategically. This section, covering two pages, contains:

- a mission statement
- a statement of vision and values in regard to the countryside
- a statement of principles
- three broad aims for the next decade in draft form, which are emerging from the new strategy mentioned above
- four key themes for the current plan
- a statement of priorities
- statutory duties.

The mission is:

> to safeguard and enhance the quality of England's countryside for future generations, and to enrich people's lives through appreciation and enjoyment of the countryside.

Examples of the values are a countryside that:

- is rich and diverse in physical character
- provides a sense of freedom and scope for personal development and health

- is economically and socially prosperous.

These values define an end result which is desired, whereas the principles make statements with more immediate implications and of more immediate applicability if those end results are to be achieved. Examples of principles are:

- actions that could cause irreversible environmental damage should be avoided so that future generations can inherit a countryside in at least as good condition as we did

- environmental benefits are valuable in their own right, and contribute to the prosperity of communities and individuals

- we should raise people's expectations rather than decide what is best for them, enabling individuals and communities to assess the needs of their local countryside, determine their own priorities, and set their own local agendas.

❏ Programme

This section covers 26 pages, the bulk of the plan. It contains entries for each of 28 programme areas with each area containing the following elements:

- policy objectives
- policy development and research and experimentation work
- operational delivery
- publicity and information
- key targets 1994/95
- financial allocations.

The policy development, research and experimentation, operational delivery and publicity and information sections basically provide a short description of activities and intentions in a narrative form. Examples of policy objectives are given in Figure 13.4. Some are very specific, but they also illustrate the difficulty in defining specific medium-term outcomes for some of the Commission's responsibilities. The key targets do tighten up on these objectives. Examples are quoted in Figure 13.5. In many cases they have to take the form of action plans, of tasks to be completed or milestones to be achieved. The letters in Figures 13.4 and 13.5 point to objectives and targets which relate to each other.

A. To encourage an effective planning system which prevents developments in the countryside that are incompatible with the conservation and enjoyment of the countryside and delivers those that are compatible.

B. To encourage sensitive management of farmland and woodland, so as to create and conserve high quality landscapes and wildlife habitats which people can enjoy.

C. To double the tree cover of England (to 15 per cent) by the middle of the next century.

D. To create nationally renowned routes for extensive journeys on foot, horseback or bicycle through England's finest countryside.

E. To promote the use of all suitable country parks and recreation sites as gateways to the countryside, so they facilitate public enjoyment of the wider countryside.

F. To secure National Park equivalent status for the New Forest.

G. To create community forests on the edges of towns and cities, through major environmental improvements and the makings of well-wooded landscapes for wildlife, work, recreation and education.

Figure 13.4. Examples of policy objectives.

A. To run 17 regional seminars and national briefings targeted at local authority officers and members.

B1. To grant aid 18 land acquisitions covering a total area of at least 530 hectares.

B2. To secure endorsement by London Boroughs of the Thames landscape strategy.

C. To monitor progress on indicative forestry strategies.

D1. To develop options for the future management, marketing and funding of National Trails.

D2. To create 32 km of new trail.

E. To implement the Visitor Welcome scheme.

G. To support the production of Forest plans and business plans for 9 forests.

Figure 13.5. Examples of key targets for 1994/95.

❑ Management and organisation

The section on management and organisation is 10 pages in length, but half of this is in the format of the information on programme areas, covering objectives, operational delivery and key targets for support services. The remainder brings together, at corporate level, some of the implications of the proposed programmes and resource allocations. In the words of the plan, the section:

- provides an overview of the Commission's resources
- identifies the consequences of the new planning figures
- moves on to consider areas for possible growth or reductions in budgets
- outlines our staffing strategy, and then
- sets out our management and administrative plans by programme area.

The second and third elements are obviously particularly important for the sponsoring department, and reflect the use of the plan for making the case for funding in the public expenditure survey.

❏ The appendices

There are two appendices. The first shows the financial allocations, split down by the headings in Figure 13.1, for each programme area. This brings together in one place information already shown earlier under individual programme areas. The second appendix shows figures for a range of performance indicators covering both programme work and administration. There are 67 performance indicators in total, though measurement of some did not start until April 1994.

Assessment

The Countryside Commission has now been producing corporate plans since 1982. Over this period a great deal of experience has been gained and many improvements have been introduced. In particular, there has been continuous improvement in increasing the active involvement of staff and giving the planning process a more central place in the management of the Commission. However, one lesson is that planning processes cannot stand still. There is a need for continuous improvement and it is always possible to see how the processes could be further improved. Some of the further changes under consideration are described below.

❏ A strategic plan

Although some strategic thinking has gone into the four-year corporate planning exercise, it is felt that there is a need to stand back more from time to time to take a potentially radical new look at direction and priorities. The tendency in an annual planning cycle is always to start where you are and then consider an incremental change from there rather than a step change to something completely different. Attempts to introduce more radical thinking at the consultation meeting at the analysis stage of the planning have not been particularly successful.

Business plans, which make a case for changes in policy or programmes, do help to fill the gap to some extent, but they only look at one initiative at a time. Another approach which has helped to fill the gap more successfully has involved specific value for money studies. These are undertaken as a rolling programme of about two studies a year. Each study concentrates on one particular area of activity, such as National Trails or countryside management, to examine whether the expenditure is offering good value for money, in terms of effectiveness, efficiency and economy. These studies have sometimes led to significant changes in programmes.

Business plans and value for money studies still do not give the opportunity for a fundamental review of overall priorities. It was therefore decided that the Commission should introduce a strategic plan, looking ahead ten or even fifteen years. As a purely illustrative example, such a plan could look more fundamentally at the relative priorities of areas such as National Parks, coastlines and countryside areas close to major cities. As another example, it could look at the relative priorities of interpretation facilities at major sites, education through the media, or education through schools. It is felt that a formal strategic planning exercise is needed, quite separately from the regular corporate plan to stimulate this more radical thinking.

Having decided to prepare a longer-term strategic plan, to a reasonably leisurely timescale, the Commission then speeded up the process. This was because the Secretary of State for the Environment requested a study of the possibility of a merger between the Countryside Commission and English Nature. It was felt that the strategic plan would inform this review. Some planning techniques were employed to help facilitate the process. Champions were appointed to lead working groups to identify strategic direction for specified areas of activity, SWOT analysis was used, and key success factors were identified. However, the process was somewhat rushed, and, subject to the decision taken by the Secretary of State following the study, it is felt that it would be helpful to revisit the strategy in due course in a more leisurely timescale.

❑ Commitment and involvement

The Countryside Commission staff include many who have professional qualifications and who are strongly committed ethically to the Commission's work. Experience elsewhere in the public sector suggests that such groups are not naturally committed to the concepts of corporate planning, to objective consideration of major changes in direction, to specifying objectives and targets clearly, and to rigorous monitoring of performance. The planning process can often be seen as an unnecessary administrative burden, rather than as an aid to management and to more effective performance. Clearly, the Countryside Commission has done a great deal to get people involved in the planning process and to make the plans a focal point for management of the organisation. The plans are in a form where they can be used to inform decisions on the allocation of resources and as a basis for regular monitoring of the business. Nevertheless, in some quarters there are apparently still hearts and minds to be won, a feeling that planning requires a lot of time and effort and is top heavy, a feeling that it requires information for information's sake.

The staff handbook entry certainly emphasises the central importance of corporate planning. It stresses its role in relation to partners and central Government, but it also describes its role internally:

> the internal management role referred to in the first objective centres on the need to draw together a broad programme of work devoted to a variety of themes into a corporate package, in which each strand of the work is mutually supportive, so that the overall effect is greater than the sum of the parts. Secondly, the Corporate Plan acts as the internal management instrument by which the Commission can tailor its activities to levels achievable with the financial, manpower and information resources available. Thirdly, by updating the plan a regular stock-take is made of what progress there has been in achieving strategic advances.

There is a planned, gradual decentralisation of budget responsibility to cost centres with middle management (Grade 7 level) taking on greater responsibility and accountability. It is felt that this helps to reinforce the importance of the plans at that level. Delegation of staff cost budgets in the future will take that process further. It is also the intention of the corporate planning group to take the 'show on the road' in the coming months, to explain more to people about how the planning system works, to try to break down the remaining barriers. There is also a helpline and training sessions are provided to assist people who have to provide information in the planning process. Quite clearly, staff at branch and regional head level are actively involved already, but it is felt important that more junior staff should understand how it affects them and how they can contribute. In particular, it is important that they should recognise how important their own personal forward job plans are within the planning system.

❑ Objectives and targets

The difficulty of setting specific objectives and tight targets is very evident, and to a considerable degree is inherent in the nature of the Commission's responsibilities. It is easier to set objectives and targets where an organisation delivers services directly than where it works through others. In the latter situation it is inevitable that some targets will take the form of milestones to be reached or actions to be completed by specific dates. This reflects the fact that it is very much easier for people to say what they want to do than it is to specify what the ultimate outcome ought to be. Nevertheless the Commission feel that it is important to continue working to make the objectives more specific. This will:

- further improve the clarity of future direction and purpose
- provide a firmer basis for monitoring, make the monitoring clearer and more straightforward, and thereby improve the basis for day-to-day decision-making.

Progress is certainly being made, as evidenced by the list of performance indicators in the second appendix of the corporate plan.

❑ Format of the plan

The present written plan seeks to meet, in a single document, requirements of three main audiences:

- Commission staff
- partners
- central Government.

It is something of a compromise between the differing requirements. Information on the 28 individual programmes is certainly necessary for the Commission staff, but arguably it offers too much operational detail for central Government. Similarly, the presentation of 67 performance indicators seems not to fit with the idea that sponsoring departments should concentrate their attention on a small number of key targets. It should be emphasised that this level of detail is considerably less than was provided in the past, and the Commission is moving toward less detail, as more emphasis is placed on getting the overall context right through the new strategy (prospectus).

It seems likely that, in the future, the corporate plan provided for central Government, and perhaps for partners, will concentrate more on the key themes identified in the strategic thinking. To the outside observer, it seems that it may be necessary to explain a little more of the thinking behind the key proposals in the plan, of the justification for the level of resources in the preferred option. That will also need the development of clear high-level objectives, performance indicators and targets. A strategic plan would need to fit into the model as well. The strategic plan would provide the justification for basic direction and purpose, and would identify key themes. The corporate plan would then start with the strategy and explain the high-level initiatives proposed over the medium-term to support that strategy.

One point which should be emphasised in regard to the above is the importance of a clear understanding with the sponsoring Department as to what they actually require. The Department of the Environment do issue some guidance and have offered feedback on previous plans. However, within the Department of the Environment there is a wide variety of groups with an interest in the Countryside Commission, some of which may, indeed, be interested in particular details only. This makes it difficult for the Department, too, to be clear as to its requirements. Quarterly meetings with Departmental officials, plus further informal contact, contribute to the feedback, but cannot really substitute for a more formal agreement on the appropriate format and content of the plan.

Reference

Countryside Commission (1994) *Corporate Plan (1994/95 - 1997/98)* Cheltenham, Countryside Commission

Chapter 14

Strategic management at the Civil Service College

The Civil Service College, created in 1970, became one of the first Next Steps executive agencies in 1989. Its parent department is the Office of Public Service and Science (OPSS). Its role, as set out in its framework document, is to provide training for civil servants, in support of which it may also offer consultancy services and offer services to the wider public sector and the private sector.

By the time it became an executive agency it had been required to recover all its costs by charging for its courses, except that there was a central payment which contributed towards its accommodation costs. This payment will have been phased out completely by April 1995. No Government department is required to use the College's courses. The College has to compete for business with other providers of training, including departments' own training sections. In fact it has a very small share of the total civil service training market, less than 5%, but this reflects the fact that the College does not generally offer training in skills for the more junior grades. At senior management level the College's market share is more like 40%.

The College has a residential centre at Sunningdale Park near Ascot in Berkshire and a non-residential centre in central London. Sunningdale Park has thirteen teaching suites and about 260 bedrooms, the London centre has six teaching suites. In addition to offering courses at these centres, the College provides tailored courses on clients' own premises, known as single client business, which in 1993/94 accounted for around 40% of the College's activity.

The College has a staff of about 250 full-time equivalents, of which between 90 and 100 are teaching staff. In addition, there are several hundred associates who make a major contribution to the teaching. The organisational structure is illustrated in Figure 14.1. The College is divided into eight business groups, each headed by a Director. Each Director has a Business Manager who heads the administrative section. Every member of teaching staff is allocated to a business group for formal line management purposes, but their time may be divided between a number of business groups for the delivery of courses. Some Directors also take responsibility for support service functions within the College.

The management board, known as the Business Executive, consists of the Chief Executive, the Director of Studies, all Business Group Directors, the Head of

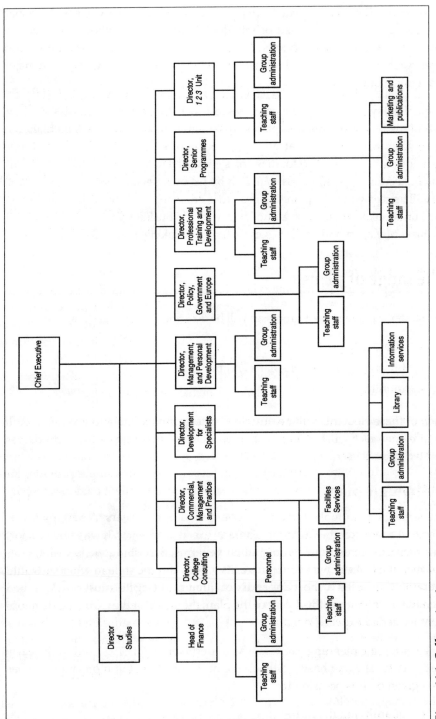

Figure 14.1. College structure.

Finance and the Head of Facilities Services. There is also a College Advisory Council, chaired by the Head of the Home Civil Service, whose membership consists of senior civil servants, including some Permanent Secretaries and Agency Chief Executives, and representatives of private sector industry and major academic institutions.

Responsibility for the planning processes rests with the Director of Studies. Broadly, 20% of his time is allocated to planning, though this percentage will be higher in those years when a new strategic plan is being produced. There are no full-time planning staff, but the Director of Studies is assisted in the planning activity by the Chief Executive's personal assistant and by his own personal secretary/assistant. As will be seen when the planning process is described, most of the planning activity is undertaken at business group level, with the Business Group Directors, their Business Managers and heads of service functions taking most of the responsibility.

The range of plans

The strategic management processes will be described under three main headings:

- strategic plan
- business plan, course plans and budgeting
- monitoring.

Each of these elements will be described briefly immediately to give an overall picture. Then each will be looked at in more detail, with descriptions of approaches and techniques used.

❑ Strategic plan

The strategic plan looks forward over a period of five years. A new plan was prepared soon after the College became an executive agency. It was a fairly short document, expressed mostly in qualitative terms, describing the key directions in which the College wished to move, its values and the style in which it would operate. It included a short appendix of numerical targets, most of which had been met by about the third year of the plan; the speed of the College's development exceeded expectations.

A new strategic planning exercise was undertaken in late 1993 and in the early part of 1994. The emphasis is still on the basic direction, but more attention has been given on this occasion to:

- quantifying the future

- identifying programmes of work to achieve change.

The former was felt to be necessary particularly in order to check financial viability, given both the loss of the remaining central payment and also a formal mandate to look at the possibility of becoming a trading fund. Moving to trading fund status has implications for methods of accounting and financial targets, so the strategic plan must provide a baseline against which to calculate the financial implications of becoming a trading fund.

The framework document requires the College's strategic plan to be available in the library of the Houses of Parliament, in other words it is a public document.

❑ Business plan

In the past, business planning has only looked one year ahead. As from 1994, however, a three-year horizon has been adopted, primarily for two reasons. The first is to tie it in more closely with the three-year forward look of the public expenditure survey. Without a three-year plan, the financing requirements input to the public expenditure survey tended to be a bit notional and based largely on what was actually happening at present, particularly by way of capital programmes. Now that the major refurbishment of the Sunningdale site is nearing completion, more thought needs to be given to a schedule of replacement and updating requirements over the coming few years.

The second reason for moving towards a three-year horizon is to take account of the programme of initiatives identified in the strategic plan. Some of these will need to be progressed over a period of more than a year and there was a wish to ensure that these projects and programmes were properly incorporated into the business plan, to help ensure that action actually materialises.

❑ Course plans and budgets

Budgets and targets for the year immediately ahead are now formally tied to the business plan, they represent the first year of that plan. However, as far as the business groups are concerned, it is necessary to check that the plans for courses fully support the targets in the business plan. A good deal of effort has to be put into course planning because of the needs to:

- produce a prospectus
- match the course plans to the availability of accommodation
- avoid date clashes for teaching staff.

Because of the interrelationships between business groups, this very detailed planning has to be co-ordinated centrally.

❏ Monitoring

The College's management information system is known as the Training Management System (TMS). It is a database system, which combines booking, invoicing and information. It allows individual managers access to reports on business results and information on bookings at any time. A formal business report, summarising results at College-wide level, is produced and presented to the Business Executive monthly. This report currently concentrates on the key targets which have to be reported quarterly to the Office of Public Service and Science.

The strategic planning process

This description concentrates on the strategic plan which has just been prepared. In fact, at the time of writing, the written version to be submitted to the Office of Public Service and Science has not quite been completed. The process was broken into stages:

- information gathering
- management team two-day meeting
- appraisal of main options
- preparation of strategic statements by each business group
- review of overall results and final conclusions.

❏ Information gathering

The first step taken was the preparation of an information pack prior to the management team's (Business Executive's) two-day meeting. This pack was 120 pages of A4 paper in length, though in practice it was a little less demanding than it might appear because of the layouts adopted. So what did this information consist of?

First, the Director of Studies interviewed a group of key stakeholders in the Office of Public Service and Science. This interview followed a structured agenda, a series of discussion questions on the group members' views of the College performance and on the ways in which they felt that the College should be moving in future. They also offered views on trends in the market for training. There was scope for the participants to add further ideas outside the agenda for the discussion if they wished.

Secondly, there was a similar discussion at a meeting of the College Advisory Council, only on this occasion there was no structured agenda and each member of the Council was invited to express views on how markets would change and how the College needed to change. The notes of this meeting and of the meeting with stakeholders were written up as fully as possible.

The College is fortunate to have access to the responses to a large number of questionnaires issued to course participants. In addition to the course assessment forms issued to every student, about one student in fifteen receives a questionnaire covering all aspects of the College's service, the teaching, the accommodation, the catering and the support service. The results from these questionnaires over the previous three years were analysed and included in the information pack. The task of producing this analysis was given to the Head of Facilities Services.

The fourth section of the information pack covered trends in the external market. There were a few facts established from published statistics, but much of the information in this section came from market research, in particular an on-going survey of training trends in which the College buys a share. This section was compiled mostly by the College's Head of Marketing.

Section five constituted an analysis of past trends from the College's own TMS. This analysis was undertaken by the Head of Finance, and covered items such as:

- the balance of demand between open courses and single client business
- the balance of demand between different locations, Sunningdale, London and elsewhere
- income per student day
- average course lengths
- demand from the individual largest customers
- trends in demand from different grades of civil servant
- trends by gender
- trends in the average number of students per course
- trends in course cancellations
- course assessment scores.

There was also some cross-analysis, for example, how course assessments varied with course length. This analysis gave rise to a dilemma; it showed that students generally found longer courses the most satisfying, but the demand was increasingly concentrated on shorter courses.

As the final contribution to the information pack, each business group was asked to undertake a product life cycle analysis of its own portfolio of courses, with an accompanying commentary. The results were aggregated by the Director of Studies, to present a College-wide picture.

This information pack is felt to have helped considerably in focusing debate at the Business Executive's two-day meeting, in that it:

- pointed up very clearly some issues which would need to be addressed
- helped to minimise the scope for debating 'facts'.

While this information pack was being prepared, six focus groups of members of College staff were organised and facilitated by College lecturers. It was deliberate that no 'representative' of management would be present, so that people would not feel inhibited. There were separate focus groups for lecturers, for course administration staff and for support services staff, to try to ensure that the opinions of each group would be properly represented in the conclusions. Each group undertook both a PEST analysis and a SWOT analysis. Should the outcome of these analyses be included in the information pack? In the event, it was decided that these results would have more impact if presented to the Business Executive after they had done a similar analysis themselves.

❏ Management team two-day meeting

The outcome required from this two-day meeting was a list of strategic issues which had to be addressed, together with a view on how each issue should be taken forward. Consideration was given to commencing with a mandates analysis and a formal stakeholder analysis. However, in the event, it was decided that this was not necessary, given the outcome of the discussion with the College Advisory Council and the representatives of the Office of Public Service and Science and the information available from customer surveys. Instead, we moved straight to an expression of the core objectives, expressed basically in the form of bullet points as follows:

- continuous improvement in learning, facilities and customer service offered, to compare to the best available
- break even financially
- continuing efficiency improvement
- high penetration of market of civil servants at Grade 7 and above
- increase volume of non-civil servants
- maintain numbers of students in development schemes

- increase numbers of students attending accredited courses.

In addition, the discussions with stakeholders had suggested the following objectives which might be thought of as supporting objectives:

- achieve 'Investor in People' status
- a viable consultancy business
- wider geographical presence
- maintain high utilisation of main sites.

These core objectives then provided the basis for a PEST analysis and SWOT analysis, following which the conclusions were compared with those of the staff focus groups, and attention turned to the identification of issues. There were nineteen, which presented something of a problem. They could not all be addressed. However, on examination there were many cases where resolution of the issue was not immediately critical to the development of a strategy. It was decided that most of the issues should be left to be tackled systematically through the business planning process, which would allocate responsibilities, set dates for resolution of the issue, and then pick up the results and incorporate them into targets. Examples could be the need for less cumbersome financial systems, and the need for new and clearer information technology and marketing strategies. In other cases we needed to take a view on the outcome required, with some checks on feasibility, but did not need immediately to work out exactly how the results would be achieved. An example of this was the need to reduce costs in some areas, where, from benchmarks, we knew what ought to be attainable but needed to undertake detailed project work in order to establish the specific changes required.

In the light of the discussion, it was decided that the requirement in the strategic plan was to prioritise the issues and to resolve a few fundamental ones covering:

- single client and open business
- the markets in which we should seek to expand or contract
- our geographical presence
- the character and skills of our staff and the mix of College staff and associates
- our core values.

The method chosen to resolve these was to build four scenarios for the College in the year 2000. Each scenario would cover each of the elements listed immediately above, to build an internally consistent picture. For example, a particular view of the markets to be expanded would be combined with the staff skills and values appropriate to those markets. At the end of the two days, the skeletons of these scenarios had been constructed.

❑ Appraisal of the options

After the management team meeting, the scenarios were built up with a one to two page description of each. These were then put back to the management team for comment.

It was decided that all staff would be invited to take part in a weighting and ranking exercise, to help to inform the decision. Four sessions were organised and, in total, about 120 staff took part. In small groups of three, they went through the weighting and ranking, the scores of each option against each criterion were quickly entered on the computer and shown on a large screen. The facilitator talked through the results, giving people an opportunity to comment and question, but generally people were very happy with the interpretation of the results.

The management team then spent half a day doing the same exercise, but without knowing the results of the staff groups. It turned out that the management team came up with a different answer! The two answers were compared in detail, and it turned out that the difference arose largely because the management team had felt that the staff would view certain issues rather differently than they did. In the light of that, a particular scenario was selected as the basis for further work.

❑ Group strategic statements

Individual business groups and service providers were then asked to produce strategic statements, to show how they would propose to deliver their work to contribute to the chosen scenario. There was a requirement to submit some broad figures on volumes, incomes, costs, location of activity, staffing requirements and so on, so that we could check the overall viability of the total picture against the core objectives proposed earlier. The groups were given two months to do this work. No specific method of working was demanded, but most did involve their staff in generating the proposals.

❑ Review of results

The strategic statements were presented to the management team, together with an assessment of the results for the College as a whole. In the light of the discussion, which served to highlight some problems of overlap between the groups, some of the business groups were asked to revisit their strategic statements and make some amendments. When this was done, the service provider groups were asked to confirm whether their original statements were still valid and invited to make any necessary amendments. This then constituted the final strategy and a ten page summary was then prepared. It was discussed at the College Advisory Council. It was also distributed to every member of staff, together with an invitation to attend a meeting on any of six dates with the Director of Studies to discuss it. Some useful points were made in these meetings and are reflected in the written version being prepared for submission to the Office of Public Service and Science.

The written document will essentially be a description of the conclusions reached at each stage of the process described and of the reasons for those conclusions. It will lead up to a final description of the key strategies and of what the College is aiming to be and achieve, including a view of the targets in broad terms and of the College's resource requirements and likely financial position. The strategic statements of the separate groups will be retained as internal documents, a framework contributing each year to the assessment of their business plan proposals and of results; they will not be part of any published document.

The business planning process, course planning and budgets

The business planning process commences in April each year, immediately after the year end, with a review of the previous year's performance. This review is intended to identify the key issues which have to be addressed in the business planning process, and to establish guidelines for that process. These guidelines would normally include some indicative quantitative targets for each group. However, this year this was not felt to be necessary, in view of the fact that so much work had been done on strategic planning. The guidelines were simply that the business plans should be compatible with the agreed strategic statements and should move the groups in the direction set out in those statements.

The conclusions reached from this review also provide the basis for a submission to the Office of Public Service and Science (OPSS) regarding the College's public expenditure needs, for OPSS to take into account in their early discussions with the Treasury in the public expenditure survey.

An important element of the process at this stage is to agree a timetable for the key steps in the remainder of the process. This is vital because of the interrelationships between the groups, they must all move in step with each other. There are also key points in the process when figures from groups have to be added together to see how things look from the College-wide point of view. This can only be done if everyone has submitted their figures. The business planning process has to be managed as tightly as possible, as a project.

❏ Group planning

The next stage, covering about ten weeks, is for the individual business groups and service provider groups to prepare their business plans. A great deal of emphasis has been placed on trying to make these top-down plans, not in the sense of plans imposed from the top, but in the sense of thinking through what the Groups ought to be doing, and then thinking about the resources required to achieve that. In the past, the emphasis has been on course planning for the year ahead, and this tempts people to concentrate their thoughts on a bottom-up process, in the sense of incremental change, how can we do something more or something a bit different with the resources which we have? The three-year horizon has certainly helped to turn people's attention more to the need to make significant changes.

❏ Review and bilaterals

In early to mid-July all of the group plans are submitted to the Director of Studies, who adds all the key figures together and produces an overview of the position reached to the management team. We would not normally expect there to be substantive discussion at this stage, unless a significant College-wide issue was emerging This overview is primarily for information and forms the background for a series of bilateral meetings between the Director of Studies and the Directors or Heads of each Group. The outcome of these bilaterals is a set of proposed medium-term objectives for up to three years ahead and a set of proposed targets for coming year.

At this point, it is reasonable to write up the business plan for submission to the Office of Public Service and Science. Although there may be some changes to individual group plans in the light of the detailed course planning, these should be manageable internally. This would make the plan available to the department in time for the later stages of discussions in the public expenditure survey. This year the submission of this plan to OPSS has been left until October, but consideration will be given in future to producing it for the end of July.

❏ Course planning

The targets then form the basis for business groups to move ahead with detailed course planning. This is real bottom-up planning; course planning should be designed to meet the proposed targets, but at the same time it should be used to validate those targets, to 'prove' that it should be possible to meet the targets. It should be emphasised here that the detailed course planning produces the programme of courses to be included in the College's prospectus, but it also includes a careful assessment of how much non-scheduled work it ought to be feasible to achieve in particular subject areas. Although the full details of these courses have to be submitted to the Director of Studies, this is because the details are needed to allow the central scheduling of courses to try to optimise the use of space and teaching staff. The details are not questioned, they are considered a matter for the groups themselves, the issue of concern to the Director of Studies and the Chief Executive is whether, in the light of the detailed bottom-up planning, the Group Directors are able to confirm acceptance of the targets suggested earlier. It should be pointed out that these targets cover costs as well as outputs. If the targets are agreed, they and the levels of resources are formally confirmed in letters from the Chief Executive.

Monitoring

A business report, covering performance against key targets for the College as a whole and for each business group, is presented to the Business Executive at its monthly meeting. It is always treated as one of the major items on the agenda. This report also includes information on forward bookings, and is operating well as a basis for discussion of current performance on the key dimensions of volumes of business, volumes of different types of business, quality assessments, and finance.

There is, in addition, a project group which monitors progress with cross-group projects, allowing reports back to the Business Executive. Conclusions of each project are reported back to the Executive for formal approval.

One of the issues with the monitoring system is that it is strongly geared to the one year ahead business planning of the past. The medium-term objectives now developed for both business and service provider groups go beyond the quantitative targets monitored at present. As a result we shall need to start monitoring milestones, changes in approach, changes in style of working, and more. It will not be appropriate to look at these each month; progress will tend to be steady rather than rapid in many cases. At present, it has not been decided how to tackle this, but it might be more appropriate to approach it through quarterly meetings with individual Group Directors perhaps backed up by more qualitative reports at quarterly intervals to the Business Executive.

Business reporting has concentrated very heavily in the past on the results of the business groups, the groups which actually deliver the training and consultancy and which are primarily responsible for earning the income. Obviously, this is critical to the business, and must continue to occupy a central place in the monitoring. The costs of the service provider groups are also monitored in the monthly Business Report. The next step is to introduce into that report some performance information on the levels of service offered by those service providers to their customers, many of whom will be internal customers. From a strategic point of view this is important, because these services play an important role in facilitating the effective longer-term performance of the business groups.

Assessment

The Civil Service College is a relatively small organisation in terms of staff numbers. This has allowed a higher level of participation of staff at all levels than would be feasible in a larger organisation. This is a good thing, because the college employs a high percentage of people who, by the very nature of their work, tend to be articulate and wish to be involved. The level of participation has been strongly welcomed. The approach to the weighting and ranking exercise was particularly successful. People found it fun, they felt they all had a voice (which would not have been the case in an open discussion) and they were grateful to see their results played back to them before they left the meeting. It remains to be seen to what extent this is carried forward into commitment to the strategy. The delay in writing up the final version of the strategy may result in some loss of momentum.

The business planning process continues to develop. The 'discipline' improves year by year as people see how the various contributions need to slot together. People also grow more accustomed to the work involved. The message here seems to be not to try to be too ambitious when first introducing planning systems. It is important to recognise that people learn by doing. In the early stages the planning team may need to do more of the work centrally than they would like, they will certainly need to help people with their plans, but it is important not to take the easy route and do everything centrally for ever. Another lesson from the college's experience is that it takes time to get people to raise their sights towards step changes from incremental changes. The involvement of people in the strategic planning, particularly the requirement on each group to produce a strategic statement, seems to have helped significantly to raise the sights towards step changes.

It does appear that there has, in the past, been a gap between the longer-term vision of the strategic plan and the one year targets which formed the basis of in-year monitoring and control. To some extent the gap was filled by cross-group projects, but these tended to be short term in themselves. The major longer-term project was the refurbishment of the Sunningdale site, and this was the prime strategic preoccupation. Now that project is nearing completion, there will be other changes which will need to be implemented to assure long-term success, changes which may spread over more than a year. The introduction of three-year business planning should help to ensure that such projects are identified, then managed and monitored in a systematic way.

Finally, while business planning must operate to a firm schedule if it is to link effectively to the public expenditure cycle and, indeed, to the financial year, strategic planning does need to be rather more leisurely. It is not possible to see at the beginning exactly how it will proceed, to predict how many issues will be identified, how much effort will need to be put into resolving them. This has to be managed as a flexible project. Progress needs to be reviewed regularly, and the management team needs to be prepared to consider from time to time what the next steps should be, and how the process should proceed.

Index

T

U

V

W